TURN THIS CONVERSATION AROUND

ALSO BY BETH WONSON

Mastering Feedback: Everything You've Never Been Told About How to Give Feedback

Let Go of the Rock! A New Look at the Dynamics of Self-Management

An Everyday Guide to Joy & Abundance: A New Approach to Living with Ease

TURN THIS → CONVERSATION ← AROUND

THE 4-STAGE PROCESS FOR COMMUNICATION WITH CONNECTION

BETH WONSON
Founder of Navigating Challenging Dialogue®

with ANDREA BUCHTEL

Copyright © 2022 Beth Wonson
All Rights Reserved.
Printed in the United States of America
First Edition

No part of this publication may be reproduced or transmitted in any form or by any means, mechanical or electronic, including photocopying or recording, or by any information storage and retrieval system, or transmitted by email without permission in writing from the author. Reviewers may quote brief passages in reviews. Neither the author nor the publisher assumes any responsibility for errors, omissions, or contrary interpretations of the subject matter herein. Any perceived slight of any individual or organization is purely unintentional. Brand and product names are trademarks or registered trademarks of their respective owners. To maintain confidentiality, names have been changed throughout the book.

Cover Design: Martine Cameau
Interior Design: Francine Platt, Eden Graphics, Inc.
Production and Editing: Karen K Christoffersen
Contributing Editor: Andrea Buchtel
Developmental Editor: Ginger Moran

Library of Congress Cataloging-in-Publication Data
Names: Wonson, Beth, author. Buchtel, Andrea, editor.
Title: Turn This Conversation Around: The 4-Stage Process for Communication with Connection by Beth Wonson with Andrea Buchtel
Identifiers: ISBN 978-1-7364589-3-8 (paperback), ISBN 978-1-7364589-4-5 (ePub)
Library of Congress Control Number: 2022915664

Elizabeth Wonson, 5150 Fair Oaks Blvd. STE 101-166, Carmichael, California 95608
www.ncdpublishing.com

This book is dedicated to
the hundreds of clients who have shown courage and vulnerability
as they've learned the tools of Navigating Challenging Dialogue® and
continue practicing NCD as a methodology to communicate, lead,
and build healthy relationships. I'm honored to have worked with you.

TABLE OF CONTENTS

Part I: Turn This Conversation Around 1

    CHAPTER 1: Welcome to Navigating Challenging Dialogue® 3

    CHAPTER 2: Where My Journey Began 7

Part II: The Foundation of NCD 23

    CHAPTER 3: Preparing Ourselves for Change 25

    CHAPTER 4: Shifting Your Lens on Communication 29

    CHAPTER 5: Communication Challenges Are Everywhere 33

    CHAPTER 6: Why Bad Communication Happens 41

    CHAPTER 7: Self-Protection and the Amygdala 45

    CHAPTER 8: Disrupting the Amygdala Reaction 49

    CHAPTER 9: Healthy Conflict is Necessary 57

    CHAPTER 10: Anger Plays a Role in Self-Coaching 65

Part III: The Principles of NCD 55

    CHAPTER 11: Be Aware of the Energy You Bring to the Room 69

    CHAPTER 12: The Only Person I Can Manage is Myself 73

    CHAPTER 13: Grace is in the Space 77

    CHAPTER 14: That's Fascinating 81

    CHAPTER 15: Curiosity is the Pathway to Empathy 85

    CHAPTER 16: You Can Only See the World Through Your Own Lens 87

    CHAPTER 17: Trust Is Built One Conversation at a Time and One Experience at a Time 91

    CHAPTER 18: At the End of the Day, Everyone Just Wants to be Seen and Heard ... 93

PART IV: The NCD Process 97

    OVERVIEW: **The Framework** 99

    HANDS-ON: **Practicing the NCD Process** 103

    STAGE 1: **Start with the Story** 105

    STAGE 2: **Sifting for Facts** 113

    STAGE 3: **Shaping the Dialogue** 127

    STAGE 4: **Sharing What You've Prepared** 135

PART V: Seeing the NCD Process Applied 145

    LORINDA'S STORY: **Wanting to Change Someone's Behavior** 147

    TONY'S STORY: **Feeling Pressure from Many Directions** 151

    RAYMOND'S STORY: **Building Trust** 153

    SHASTA'S STORY: **Strengthening Connection** 157

    BETH'S STORY: **A Mercurial Manager** 159

PART VI: Sustaining Your Practice 163

    THE NCD MANTRAS: **Principles to Guide You** 165

    SURPRISE DIALOGUES: **A Different Conversation** 167

    RESOURCES: **Support Your Practice** 169

    IN CLOSING: **Where We Go from Here** 171

Acknowledgments 172

About the Author 173

PART I

TURN THIS
CONVERSATION
AROUND

CHAPTER 1

WELCOME TO NAVIGATING CHALLENGING DIALOGUE®

Courage starts with showing up and letting ourselves be seen.

— BRENÉ BROWN

How we communicate with each other is vital to human existence. We need each other to innovate, solve complex problems, thrive, and even develop our best selves. For this, clear communication is essential.

Yet, how communication has changed over the past several decades has created a dangerous trajectory for our human existence. We have become disconnected from each other even though we must depend on each other.

It is not entirely our fault.

We are working against our brain's innate desire to protect us from perceived threats to our beliefs, values, and sense of self. This protection mechanism was helpful back in the days when the saber tooth tiger was trying to eat our babies. Nowadays, it's more likely to warn us away from psychological threats that impact ego, confidence, reputation, values, or our sense of belonging.

We've all experienced communication where we've felt vulnerable or defensive. In today's world, many of us face an increasing number of emotionally charged conversations. Those emotions are usually a result of psychological threats which are very real to us, but often invisible to outsiders. These threats impact our thoughts, emotions, and ultimately the actions we choose to take.

It's human nature to dig in and try to find a way through challenging conversations while simultaneously grasping onto what we believe. It's often the urge to be heard and understood that leads to conflict and damaged relationships. Sometimes, everyone walks away feeling bad.

This book is about turning those conversations around and engaging in ways that create connections and get results.

I'm sharing with you the tools that I have acquired, learned, and practiced as I transformed my communication and leadership. This is a practice I call Navigating Challenging Dialogue® (NCD). Using real-world examples, I'll demonstrate the exact steps that will change how you manage yourself, especially in tough conversations.

You'll learn to transform the thoughts that activate feelings of being in danger before communication and healthy conflicts are derailed. Through the practice of NCD, you can regain your innate ability to connect with others, have positive, productive conversations, and increase trust—even when you may not agree.

By practicing NCD, I've learned to be a steward of healthy conflict. I now approach challenges with curiosity and wonder, gaining perspective on how others see an issue and how they came to believe what they do.

On my journey, a few principles have stood out as being essential to relationship building, empathy, and trust. I keep these principles front and center in my mind as I engage with others. When you integrate these principles, you will find ease and grace, even in the most challenging communications.

I've formalized my tools into a 4-Stage framework I call the NCD Process. Follow the process to identify the thoughts your brain uses to protect you and which activate feelings of danger. You can then evaluate their validity or relevance before they show up in communication, actions, and conflicts.

The four stages can be summarized as:

- **Stage 1**—*The Story*
- **Stage 2**—*Sifting for Facts*
- **Stage 3**—*Shaping the Dialogue*
- **Stage 4**—*Sharing What You've Prepared*

Within this process, you'll learn to explore the stories that make up your lens on the world. This is a practice to question your desire to be right and to become curious without judgment about the unique lens that *others* see through.

The real-world scenarios, from me and my clients, illustrate how to apply the process to a variety of situations. While most of my clients are looking to change things at work or with their team, they find that NCD is just as powerful in their personal lives.

The NCD Process is not just a business tool. It's a life tool that we all benefit from using.

When we, as a society, are better able to deploy the tools of NCD, we will also be better able to solve challenging problems and innovate new ideas. We'll develop more empathy, trust, and connection with those around us. All these skills are essential for us to thrive collectively.

My hope is that by reading this book and learning what underlies the simple framework, you will find ease and peace in your life and in your relationships at work and at home.

CHAPTER 2

WHERE MY JOURNEY BEGAN

We came into this life with the authentic knowledge that we are ultimately responsible for our emotional journey.

— BETH WONSON

I'D BEEN TRYING TO SCORE a meeting with a very influential consultant in my area. It had taken me months. I was just starting out in my business, and everyone told me I just had to meet with this guy, Robert. After months of emailing and asking for a coffee with Robert, his assistant had finally set up an appointment for us to meet.

I was excited. I hoped the connection with this influential person could open several doors for my budding business.

After what felt like a lifetime of waiting, the day of the meeting finally arrived. I was looking forward to our time together and all I might learn from this successful business owner. We were scheduled to meet at 11:00 a.m. As I was blow-drying my hair, a text dropped in from his assistant.

"Robert is at the coffee shop. He has another appointment at the top of the hour. Are you on your way?" she said.

I was not on my way. I was in my pajamas. I checked the time. It was 9:15. I checked my calendar. My appointment was for 11:00. I had a carefully calibrated 20 minutes to get ready to leave. It would take 25 more just to get there. I went into panic mode. I felt my shaking hands get sweaty. My heart felt like it was beating out of my chest.

Those old familiar tapes started running in my head:

"Beth, you always screw things up."

"You are horrible at keeping dates and times straight."

"You really blew it now."

"You aren't even worthy of this meeting."

I was overwhelmed with feelings of shame and embarrassment.

Then I remembered to breathe, to calm myself down. I knew reacting from a place of anxiety, fear, and shame would not help me solve this problem.

I took several deep breaths. Once I felt my heart rate return to normal, I looked for the original email exchanges I had with the assistant.

She had written, "Robert can meet with you on May 5 at 11:00 a.m. at the Black Horse Cafe."

I had written back, "Great. Thank you. Confirmed in my calendar for 11:00 a.m. on May 5th."

Instantly my panic turned to anger. I remember thinking, "How could she have screwed this up? Didn't she know I'd been waiting for this meeting for a month? What is wrong with her?"

I could not wait to let her and her boss know that she was wrong. I had not mistaken the time. She had screwed up. I was right. My rage was justified. Who wouldn't be angry?

I was getting ready to message her when Robert reached out via text.

"I'm sorry. My assistant just discovered that she sent each of us different times for our coffee. I have to run, but I owe you and she will get something set up this week."

I had just barely averted business and social disaster. Rage-texting my "rightness" would have sabotaged what I wanted to achieve from this meeting. If I had let the assistant be the recipient of all my uncomfortable shame and embarrassment, I likely would never have had another meeting with Robert. After all, who wants to do business with someone who reacts so emotionally to a simple mix-up? And who knows what they would have said to others in the community about my reaction to a simple mistake? Who wants to collaborate with someone who tries to relieve their discomfort by attacking another?

Once we had the new date and time sorted out, I was able to sit for a minute and reflect on my own reactions in this situation.

My biggest question for myself was, "Why am I experiencing these feelings of shame, incompetency, and unworthiness again?" And even more importantly, "What can I do to move beyond these feelings?"

Part of my answer lies in understanding what was modeled for me as a child.

My parents always had a side hustle. My dad cared for gardens and managed a greenhouse. They had an ice cream and hot dog stand next to our home. Right before I was born, Dad quit his full-time job overseeing large, industrial steam furnaces and declared to my mother, "I'm done working for other people. We are opening a florist and greenhouse business."

They were hugely successful. The business became like a member of our family. My parents loved their business and talked morning, noon, and night about strategy, sales, and ideas. All five of us kids grew up helping in the business.

After school, I was never in childcare. Instead, I just tagged along with my dad every day when he went to the flower growers to buy bundles of fresh-cut orchids, roses, carnations, and chrysanthemums. I rode shotgun as he made his rounds delivering bouquets and baskets to customers. In the spring, I was there alongside him as he tended to customers' gardens on their vast seaside estates.

I loved these times with my dad. As a little girl, I couldn't have imagined how much his work ethic, philosophy, and approach to life would impact who I'd become.

My dad was a bit of a hothead. While he was never physically violent towards others, he committed a great deal of emotional violence against himself. He did this with his self-doubt, self-rage, and vulnerability.

My mom was his accomplice and enabler. Her love and commitment to him translated into tremendous efforts to prevent my father from getting "worked up."

This is how it played out. When dad was "in a mood," he wallowed in his fears and insecurities (we called this "fretting"). My mom did whatever she could to keep a calm environment. In these moments, I learned to help by not saying anything that would be upsetting to my dad.

This is the approach I learned for love and life.

For example, I remember when I was about 10 years old, my mom and I went shopping for new shoes. The pair I fell in love with were real leather loafers. Mom liked them too. She bought them for me. When we left the store, she turned to me and said in a stern voice, "We will not tell Dad how much these cost. It will just get him worked up!"

The cost of my shoes, a seemingly insignificant piece of information, would get his head spinning with fearful thoughts. He'd slide down a rabbit hole and start what I call "future tripping." The cost of the shoes would lead to my father worrying if we could afford the cost of heating oil. What if our greenhouses, filled with the tender new seedlings for next year, dropped in temperature and the plants were lost? What if it snowed on Valentine's Day and the orders for hundreds of dozens of roses couldn't be delivered? What if there was another depression and we needed the shoe money to pay for food? What if he couldn't provide for us?

My dad's emotional reactions and my mother's hard work to ensure he would not get upset were lessons that I have had to work hard to undo in my own relationships. I must remind myself that others are whole and capable and will benefit from managing their own emotional reactions. That is not my job!

My dad had several sayings that he repeated throughout my life. Many of these have served me well in my career and with my own family.

"If you watch the pennies, the dollars take care of themselves."

"Your most difficult customer can become your best customer if you do the right thing."

My father had a few other sayings which he repeated over and over. These simple words drove me to be competitive and ambitious. I'd spread myself too thin, try to please others rather than take care of myself, and generally behave in ways very similar to him. These words, his words, became some of my unspoken rules for work and life.

Here are a few sayings that still play over and over in my thoughts in my dad's gravelly voice, even now, more than fifty years later.

"Beth, you've got to have the push."

"Beth, work along now. You've always got to work a little harder than the other guy."

"Beth, there's no time for vacations. Every place has trees, houses, and streets just like we do. It's better to work hard and stay ahead."

"Beth, keep your eye on the big guys uptown. Copy their ideas so that you can be competitive."

"Beth, competition is the best thing for business. It keeps you on your toes. If you work hard, you will come out ahead."

You can probably see the theme here: you must work hard, you must always try to get ahead, and you must compete, compete, compete!

My adult life became about always rushing and being busy so I could "keep ahead of the other guy." I became a highly competitive and hard worker. I felt validated and proud when people acknowledged how hard I worked. As a young mother, I had several side hustles going all the time in addition to working full-time in my parents' business.

As my children grew, I went back to college to get my teaching certification. I worked full time and took a full complement of classes on nights and weekends. I finished my degree in record time.

In hindsight, I can see that I was likely addicted to being busy. Being busy kept the doubts and fears that haunted me at bay. What I didn't understand at the time was that I was looking outside of myself for praise, trying to dispel my own insecurities.

Frankly, it didn't work.

My need for others to validate that I was driven and ambitious was insatiable. Even now, there are times when I'm feeling vulnerable and my need for external validation flares up. When it does, I cannot find satisfaction within myself. The result is I get busy again, which leads to unnecessary drama and chaos for myself and those around me.

When I let my emotional reaction to a conversation lead me to behavior that I thought I had grown past, I remember wondering, "Why am I experiencing this again?"

How were others satisfied with steady, consistent, and reasonable progress toward their goals when I was not? My thoughts and fears drove me to keep switching gears and changing career direction. Shame and guilt compounded my feelings of being unsuccessful. Trying to outrun my own negative self-talk, thoughts, and emotions was chaotic and eventually led to burnout.

By the time my marriage was on the rocks, I had been working as a public school administrator in my hometown. My life felt like it was so exposed. My nerves were raw. Like my mother, I wanted to make everything okay for everyone else. My work became consuming. The flaws in public education that allowed kids to fall through the cracks were overwhelming for me.

I knew I needed to pause and reset, but I had no idea how to do it or where to start.

Finally, at the age of 38, I decided to make a career move—again making a change without understanding what I was running from. That was the beginning of learning about myself and understanding how my brain works.

I went barreling into my new job at a nonprofit which focused on culture change and individual empowerment in teams and organizations. I started as a customer response person who sold training, consulting, and our specialty—the installation of adventure ropes courses.

I loved my new job. We were a happy little family of workers. The headquarters was filled with people who wanted to change the world through experiential learning and adventure education. We affectionately called ourselves "the land of misfit toys." The organization was founded by former hippies and beatniks who had dreamed of a better way to empower humans to understand and use their unique strengths and talents.

I'd finally found my work home. It fed my needs. We were a close group who socialized together, worked together, and shared stories from our lives when we ate lunch together every day. There was an unspoken expectation that we could bring all our emotional baggage to the workplace. After all, we were a non-profit. We cared about people. We accepted people's flaws and just worked around them.

Emotional outbursts were not uncommon. Passionate people yelled at each other in meetings. Doors were slammed when someone stormed out. At times, decisions were made in secrecy.

Or course, I knew how to navigate these kinds of dynamics. It was as familiar as my childhood. Drama, chaos, and emotional outbursts were my comfort zone. I navigated the politics and complex relationships all the while creating opportunities for myself.

It all involved having the push!

I failed to see that all the pushing that got me recognized and promoted was taking a toll on me, both physically and emotionally. I was building a reputation for myself that wasn't as I imagined or intended.

Meanwhile, I was looking forward to the all-day staff retreat where we'd talk about the future of the organization. I had ideas! I was ready to share them in my dominant, pushy way.

My supervisor came to me a few days before that and said, "We have a very important job for you during the retreat."

Well of course they did! I had the push. I was working harder than the other guy! I was ready.

"It is important that our customers are served, and the phones are answered," she said. "So, you are who we are going to trust with that job. You will remain here for the day and take care of business."

You can imagine my emotional reaction! My insecurities and fears were activated. I was livid. I did not handle it with grace. It was only in hindsight that I realized how significantly those feelings and thoughts had hijacked my brain. I felt trapped, unable to react in any other way. I tried to protect myself from being left behind.

By the end of the day, everyone in the company was well aware that I was angry. I ranted and raved about the foolish leadership and how it was all so unfair. I appealed to everyone I could to try and get that decision overturned.

In the end, I stayed behind and covered the phones. I acted with anger and resentment, not grace. People tiptoed around me. No one ever called me on it, but I'm sure it was discussed.

One day, I sat down alone at the lunch table. The CEO came and sat next to me. He looked at me and said very calmly, "Beth, I want to share a baseball analogy with you. If you are the batter and you swing at every single pitch, your batting average will go down. You are swinging at pitches that aren't right for you. You are raising your hand and getting yourself involved in everything, even when it isn't the best use of your skills, talents, and time. Wait for the right ball to come and swing at that. You will be much more successful. And I want you to know this, we see your skills and talents. You need to see them and use them more wisely to hit the balls that are right for you."

I began to see how frustrated I had been. I didn't feel heard at meetings. My ideas weren't received as well as I thought they should be. I was swinging at every ball, and it was causing people to block me out.

I began observing how others acted in meetings. There was one colleague, Tara, who didn't say much, but when she did, people listened. Sometimes, I even felt like I had said the same thing before her, but my ideas didn't get traction. Often, I'd say things louder or stronger, hoping to be heard.

On the heels of the CEO's story, I decided to become an observer of Tara's behavior. I noticed she was always one of the last to speak when we were brainstorming, not the first, like me. I saw that she listened with deep curiosity to everyone else. She asked clarifying questions and encouraged others to keep expanding on their ideas. She didn't push to add her voice the way I did. She wasn't emotional, and she didn't take things personally. She was very humble when she was acknowledged. She was confident. I wanted to be more like her.

The team I was on was successful. I loved being part of it. We hired two different people from the outside to lead the team. Both of these professionals had limited success. The business was tough to learn. The culture was far different from the corporate world from which they had come. Many nuances made our business model tricky. There were also many people who behaved as I did, making our own path, creating our own rules, and not being held accountable because we were so good at our individual work.

After both new team leads were unsuccessful, I was told I would lead the team. I was so happy (and quite naive). I was going to work harder than the other guys. I would rock it!

I will never forget my first Thursday as the "boss." Thursdays were typically a day when we, as a team, went out to a local restaurant or pub after work and vented about management. It was our way of burning off some steam. That first Thursday, I stepped out of my new office to inquire where we were going, and everyone was already gone. It was at that moment that I realized I was now "management," and they were going to discuss me! My fears and insecurities came rushing back.

Like many who are promoted because they are good at their work, I had no idea how to handle my own emotions or how to keep them from impacting my team members. I had no mentoring, modeling, or education on what it really takes to be a great leader. I didn't realize how vulnerable, lonely, and frightening it can feel to be the leader.

One day an employee who I valued sat down in my office and said, "I feel like you are never present with me. I can't get your full attention. It is very hard to do my best work when you are distracted and emotional. I wish you'd take a breath and just be present when we talk."

I was defensive. She didn't understand! I justified my lack of availability by telling her how much pressure I was under. That same employee resigned not too long after that conversation. I was so disappointed and angry by what I perceived to be her lack of having the drive to succeed.

I prided myself on being a great multi-tasker, always busy and on the run between meetings, phone calls, and half-completed projects. I thought I was a great role model as a woman and a leader who could do it all.

Until I hit the wall.

When we don't have the self-awareness to acknowledge our emotions and their impact, they will get our attention somehow. I had made some small improvements in my approach to other people at work, but overall, I was still at the mercy of my emotions.

My big change started as a small spot on my cheek. It itched a bit. And then it started to go across my eyebrow. I began to ache. No amount of ointment or cream could soothe it. I went to the doctor and was diagnosed with shingles.

To protect an immunocompromised person in the office, I was not able to return to work. I brought my laptop home.

Of course, instead of resting, I worked even harder. My fear of not having the push and of being left out drove my inability to rest. My drive to protect myself meant that I annoyed and interrupted the employees holding down the office with my continual emails and questions.

When I think back on this situation now, I shudder. The emotional energy generated by my unchallenged fears and stories prevented the rest I needed to heal. My anticipated three weeks of leave stretched into eight weeks. I was on disability and legally could not be doing work, so they had no choice but to send someone to my house and take my laptop.

With no distraction, I was now stuck with my insecurities and vulnerabilities. I didn't know how to just be with myself.

The doctors could not get the virus under control. The evening before Thanksgiving my sister found a doctor in Boston. He specialized in this type of virus. He was contemplating admitting me to the hospital because of the risk of sepsis, which terrified me. The doctor decided to try one last round of treatment at home with strict instructions for me to actually rest and take care of myself. I decided I'd better listen.

During that time, two things happened. One, the shingles cleared up. And two, I began to question how I was leading others and myself.

I knew there had to be a better way. I needed to transform how my own past experiences, fears, inner dialogue, and emotions were impacting my present.

I realized that my primary work was learning to manage myself. My hunch was that if I could learn to manage myself and my thoughts in a clear and emotionally clean way, I could be a much healthier and more effective leader, mother, friend, partner, daughter, and sister. I could possibly even get out of the cycle of pushing for recognition and validation and find contentment.

With this awareness, I began my journey to seek a deeper understanding of how my brain worked. I studied emotional and social intelligence and how other cultures view leadership. My goal was to reduce the churn of drama and chaos in my life. I would learn to recognize what behaviors and thoughts prompted my emotional reactions—what I call emotional hotspots. Then, I could learn to manage them.

My self-study project included learning from brain scientists and experts. I began to read everything I could find on effective leadership and social and emotional intelligence. I engaged in talk therapy to understand how I formed the unwritten rules that I lived by (be competitive, have the push, work harder than the other guy). I learned how to begin creating new neural pathways that not only changed my thoughts but changed how I habitually react to those thoughts.

I came to the life-changing realization that the thoughts and fears which activate my emotional hotspots are deeply embedded in my subconscious. I learned to be curious about my reactions. I began to recognize when my emotions were interfering with clear communication and decision-making.

People noticed the shift in me. I began to blog about what I was learning and how I was applying it. My life began to feel calmer, and my relationships felt less difficult. Decision-making and problem-solving became clearcut and straightforward. My self-confidence increased. I was becoming the leader and the person I wanted to be.

When drama occurred around me, I became an observer. I no longer felt like it was my job to fix everything for everyone. I realized that they, like me, would benefit from becoming aware of how their emotions and fears were impacting their own experiences. They too had the ability to make conscious choices regarding how they wanted to be present. I learned that we are each responsible for our own happiness.

My daughters, now adults, unknowingly helped me let go of my need to be responsible for others' happiness. When they would call me to express a challenge or frustration, I would still jump into problem-solving mode. One time, my eldest daughter called me about a challenge she was facing.

"Mom, I'm so upset and mad. I want to start my medical clerk program now, but they said I must wait another whole semester due to my health," said Lily, who had taken a very bad fall and broken her back.

She was so upset. I had taken her phone call as I was walking with two colleagues through a crowded conference venue on my way to present to a packed audience.

"I can't talk right now, Lily. But let me think about it, and I will get back to you," I said.

My concern for Lily distracted me throughout the presentation because nothing was more upsetting to me than my daughters being upset. I was so accustomed to performing while distracted that the audience had no idea. I rushed to call her back as soon as I could, but the call went to voicemail.

I spent the entire night wrestling with ways to fix it. I called her the next day with my solution.

And she said, "Oh, Mom. Thanks. That was yesterday. I'm fine waiting. Can I call you back later? I'm having lunch with my friends."

I had taken her call as an emergency that I needed to fix. She had taken her call as venting to her mother. Realizing the problem, we started doing a check-in so that we were all in agreement with what was being asked.

I'd start with, "What do you need from me? Advice or just an ear to listen?"

Or the girls would start the call with, "I just want to tell you about this. There is nothing you need to do" or "I need your help, Mom."

The more I practiced these strategies, the more my life felt at ease and productive. There was far less drama and chaos to sort out.

One time, I was facilitating a meeting where there was a great deal of angst and stress between team members. One of the participants looked at me and asked, "How do you do it?"

"Do what?" I responded, even though I was certain I knew what she was asking.

"How do you stay so calm and so even-keeled when everyone else is so stressed out? You never get sucked in. I'm not even part of this, and I'm totally stressed out," she said.

"It's practice. I focus on the facts. I stay in my own business and know that the only person I can manage is myself. I am aware of my own energy and manage it in a way so that it doesn't add to the negative energy in the room. It takes practice. I didn't learn it overnight."

The new skills I'd acquired turned me from a chaotic and sometimes feared leader to a highly valued person to have around. These skills are the foundation of Navigating Challenging Dialogue. My personal experience impacted me in such a positive way that I felt certain others would benefit too. I did not want NCD to be my secret.

One day, I was in my garden pruning my giant trumpet vine when the framework for the NCD Process was downloaded into my brain. I dropped my shears, ran to my laptop, and began writing out the steps I used for getting clean and clear in my own communication.

It was time for me to begin sharing the tools I had acquired, learned, and practiced. That was in 2014, nearly twenty years after I realized that my own thoughts were getting in my way.

I am deeply grateful to my parents for all that they provided and taught me. I would not be the loving grandmother, mother, and partner I am today without their modeling of commitment to family. Everything my parents did was to provide me and my siblings with a better future than what they had. I am eternally grateful to them. I'm also deeply aware that if we don't question the thought patterns and beliefs we've inherited, we pass them on to our children. I'm grateful I can also pass along this transformative practice.

PART II
THE FOUNDATION
OF NCD

CHAPTER 3

PREPARING OURSELVES FOR CHANGE

What systems am I creating, transforming, dismantling, or replicating in my most important relationships?

— JAMES-OLIVIA CHU HILLMAN

PRACTICING NCD requires a change in your thinking patterns and actions. The work of Charles Duhigg and his book, *The Power of Habit: Why We do What We do in Life and Business,* provides great insight into why the NCD Process is effective for shifting your communication style from perpetuating drama and chaos to facilitating ease and clarity.

Duhigg maintains the reason change is difficult is because our patterns of behavior are essentially habits we've formed throughout our life. His model states that there is an event that stimulates a trigger (NCD calls this an emotional hotspot) and our reaction to that is something we've come to know will bring relief from discomfort.

This cycle applies to many personal issues such as emotional eating, substance abuse, and even drama and chaos.

My reaction was often anger. I felt justified telling the other person all the reasons that they were wrong or bad. I would then feel relieved and empowered. "I showed them!" A few minutes later, those familiar feelings of shame and regret would start to creep in. "Why am I experiencing this again? I thought I'd worked through this?"

Emotional reactions are the impulse to get rid of the discomfort we feel when something someone says or does activates an emotional hotspot in us. This is where Dughigg's model aligns with the theory of NCD.

"Emotional hotspots[1]" are our unique core triggers that are carried at an energetic level in our bodies. Some of our emotional hotspots become embedded before we have the cognitive ability to put language to feelings. Thus, talk therapy often is not helpful when addressing these core triggers.

Experts say that we can put words to feelings at about age seven. So, the experiences we have before age seven tend to be feeling-based. We don't have the kinds of language skills to verbalize and understand those early experiences as we do past age seven.

Here is an example that illustrates what I mean. Ideally, the first baby in the family has the mother's undivided love and attention. Then, the second sibling joins the family. The first child still expects their mother to respond to them in the same ways. When the older child needs or wants the mother and she responds with, "I can't pick you up. I have to hold the baby," the child experiences feelings they can't yet process. Those feelings are stored in the body as energy.

As healthy, functioning adults, we can see that the mother's response was based on facts. The newborn does not have the same level of independent functioning as the older child. The mother had to prioritize the infant over her eldest in that moment. Her response makes total sense to us. However, the negative feeling experienced by the older child can linger in the child's body and psyche.

Fast forward twenty-five years. The older child is sitting in a business meeting. The boss says, "I have a special project and

I need you, you, and you." This child, now an adult, is not included in the group for the special project.

The emotional hotspot may get activated, causing them to feel the same feeling as when their mother said, "Not now." The child within feels the discomfort of the emotional hotspot and, as Dughigg's model shows, takes an action to get a reward—the reward being removal from discomfort.

As you will see when we talk about the amygdala later, the reaction will likely come from a fight or flight response. This means that the person will either fight (defend, blame, justify) or flee (retreat, shut down, become passive-aggressive).

NCD teaches the skills of pause, reflect, and question. It does not mean that the emotional hotspot will no longer be activated. Instead, you will become familiar with what it feels like when you experience hotspots so you can pause and choose how to proceed, instead of simply allowing your body chemistry and old patterns to control you.

The NCD Process is a framework for sustainable change. However, it requires attention and intention on a continuing basis. I practice NCD every day. Occasionally old emotional hotspots activate, and I react rather than respond. Often, as I feel it happening, I pause, breathe, and use the NCD Process to show up and move forward.

---

1   You may have heard emotional hotspots referred to as triggers. Out of respect for very real mental health challenges such as Post Traumatic Stress Disorder, I don't use the word trigger. This is also a good time to mention that NCD may not be a suitable tool for conversations with people who are struggling with challenges related to mental health or cognitive function.

CHAPTER 4

SHIFTING YOUR LENS ON COMMUNICATION

*We see the world through the lens of all our experiences;
that is a fundamental part of the human condition.*

— MADELEINE M. KUNIN

YOU'VE PICKED UP THIS BOOK for a reason. Something about the title or my work has intrigued a part of you that seeks more meaningful connections, less drama and unhealthy conflict.

Some of you may have come here to discover how to get others to hear you better, to listen to you more, or simply to do what you say. You want to convince others that your thoughts, ideas, and beliefs are superior.

You won't discover those secrets in this book.

What you will learn are self-awareness and emotional self-management. By following the NCD Process, you will be focusing on yourself, not on others. For most of us, this is a giant, and often uncomfortable, shift.

Why? Because your ego's job is to reinforce to you that you are smart, in control, and right. In fact, you are an expert. Your ego encourages you to focus on where others are wrong and to prove it to them through your words and actions. Your ego's desire to maintain your perceived expert status shows up as behaviors that perpetuate unhealthy conflict.

Exploring a more easeful and peaceful way of engaging with others is often an uncomfortable process in the beginning. Like hundreds of others, you may feel some resistance.

Here are some ways to open yourself to receiving, instead of being overwhelmed by all that the practice of NCD can bring to your life.

As you read this book, be aware of how your ego responds to the information you are reading. You may observe thoughts like, "This is too simple," "This will take way too much effort," "I don't believe this," or even, "Beth is ridiculous."

Take notice of what you are reading or hearing when these thoughts show up. Don't work too hard on trying to make meaning out of it right now. Just notice your reaction. Everything will come together as you engage with the 4-Stage Process and begin integrating the tools.

Allow yourself to be an observer of communication for a little while. As you learn the principles, key concepts, and skills of NCD, observe the interactions of others around you.

Notice, without getting involved, where you see drama being created through lack of clarity. Can you see a point in the conversation where pausing to ask a few curious questions may have avoided unhealthy conflict? Notice where people become emotional, or unnecessarily take things personally.

Allow yourself to observe your life as if you were watching actors in a play. Watching a play, you never jump up and get involved in the dialogue of the actors even when you see where things are going wrong.

Allow others to find their own path forward and learn as you watch. Often the thinking patterns and errors we observe in others can reveal insights into our own thinking process.

Observing the world around you is one of the ways the practice of NCD improves your ability to have even the toughest conversations in much healthier ways. As you begin to experience more ease, you will notice places all around you where drama and conflict may be prevented.

A word of caution. As you begin experiencing less drama, chaos, stress, and unhealthy conflict in your own communication, you will begin wanting to help others do the same. However, they may or may not be ready.

The best way to introduce these concepts to others is to model the behavior you desire.

CHAPTER 5

COMMUNICATION CHALLENGES ARE EVERYWHERE

"What do you want to be when you grow up?"
"Kind," said the boy.

— CHARLIE MACKESY, *THE BOY, THE MOLE, THE FOX, AND THE HORSE*

AT THE BEGINNING of every NCD workshop, participants are asked to bring up a tough conversation they need to have but are resisting or avoiding. The pandemic and the debate over masking and vaccinations have created rifts in families and between friends and coworkers.

Here is an example of a difficult conversation one workshop participant avoided.

> "I need to have a conversation with my brother. He doesn't believe in the vaccine and says he won't get it. I'm expecting my first baby in a month, and my doctor has told me that the baby should not be around anyone who isn't vaccinated.
>
> The last time I tried to talk to my brother about getting vaccinated, he became angry and defensive. It didn't go well. That was before my doctor said not to let him see the baby unless he was vaccinated.

I know that he is fully expecting to meet his nephew. Now I must tell him he can't. But it is more than that even. I've always envisioned him and my children sharing a special bond. Now that feels impossible because he is too stubborn. I'm completely heartbroken and disappointed that he just won't do this even for me, that his own nephew isn't important enough. I have no idea how to convince him to get vaccinated."

As she shared this story, her voice cracked. Her emotion was palpable. We began working together to separate the fears, emotions, and assumptions from her story as she presented it.

After working the NCD Process, she realized that the conversation she needed to have with him wasn't actually about his choices regarding vaccination. It was about the doctor's recommendation for the health and wellness of the baby. She had what she needed to turn this conversation around from an argument about politics and vaccines to her desire for her brother to meet her baby.

She contacted me a few days later to say that she had talked to her brother, and it went like this:

"I love you, and I am eager for you to meet the baby as soon as possible. However, I've learned that only people who are vaccinated can visit in person. I am hoping that you will be able to visit."

She said that her brother responded that he would get vaccinated and that he couldn't wait to meet his new nephew.

She explained the huge change for her like this:

"In the past, I would have approached him trying to convince him to get vaccinated and telling him how hurtful it was that he would not. We would have ended up in an argument about vaccinations. This time I was very clear and kind in communicating the facts. Thank you for this, Beth. This process feels magical."

I'm always amazed at what people will do to avoid conversations where they fear they will be seen as the cause of another's disappointment or unhappiness.

This is a huge issue in the work world. Business leaders come to me all the time to help them resolve complex employee problems that easily could have been avoided had they had a direct, fact-based conversation from the beginning.

I was at a corporate headquarters to meet with an executive who was having challenges with the morale of his team. When I arrived, I walked up to the main reception desk. The woman who was behind the desk completely ignored me and continued filing papers. A door marked "Accounting Department" opened, and a woman came rushing out.

"Can I help you?" she asked.

"Yes. I'm Beth Wonson and I'm here for a meeting with William Smith."

"Okay. Have a seat and I will tell him you are here," she said as she turned and disappeared through the door.

When I met with Mr. Smith, I asked him why the person behind the desk with the receptionist sign did not greet me but a person from accounting did.

"Oh, that's Sarah. She's been here for years. She doesn't like greeting the public and frankly isn't good at it, so we put a video monitor in the accounting office, and when someone shows up, they come out and greet them," he responded.

"Have you discussed this with Sarah?"

"No. She is a really difficult person, and I don't want to make matters worse, so we just created this workaround," he answered.

I paused and waited. He said, "I really don't like upsetting people. I just want everyone to be happy."

I suddenly was completely clear on why he was having a problem with staff morale. After all, it must be quite frustrating for someone from accounting to have their concentration and workflow interrupted because the leader isn't willing to have tough conversations with his staff about the expectations for behavior and performance.

All too often I hear from people who believe they are protecting other people's feelings by not being clear and honest in their communication. The truth is that when someone avoids a tough conversation, they are only protecting themselves from having to experience another person's discomfort. In the end, avoiding tough conversations turns small challenges into larger and more complex ones.

This executive and I immediately began working on the strategies of NCD. We increased his skill, confidence, and ability to have the kinds of leadership conversations that support a healthy workplace. His employees were empowered to use their strengths and talents while supporting the goals of the company.

Clear communication leads to a satisfied team and healthy morale. Trying to keep everyone happy leads to employee frustration and leadership burnout.

Over time Sarah chose to shift her behavior and become a focused employee who understood what she needed to do to remain a part of the team.

Another time, an acquaintance came to me for coaching. She worked in a high-tech company where most people dreamed of working. She was struggling with her emotional reaction to her manager's inability to deal with his own frustrations in healthy ways. It was not uncommon for him to become red in the face, slam down the lid of his laptop, and storm out of a meeting when he was faced with feedback or dissenting opinions from his team.

She was scheduled to have a performance meeting with him in the next few days. Her concern was that his behavior was so misaligned with her values and expectations of how a leader should act, she feared she'd react badly to any feedback he had for her. She was seeking tools to be able to stay in the moment and not react with tears or anger. She didn't want to give him any excuse to call her unprofessional or to sabotage her chances of staying with the company.

In our session, we worked through the NCD Process together. The initial goal was to help her separate stories she was telling herself from the provable facts about the upcoming meeting. The second step was to give her the tools to pause and bring herself back to center when she felt emotional hotspots activating for her. Lastly, she learned to proactively identify strategies for responding with curious questions rather than defensiveness or blaming.

She called me after the meeting to tell me how it went:

"Hey, Beth. I just want you to know that even with all the work we did, my opinion of my boss still hasn't changed. He is still a big baby who can't handle his reactions. And I still have little regard for him."

We laughed about this.

"But," she added, "I was able to be present for the meeting, and I feel really good about it."

"That's great," I told her.

"I stayed curious and was able to ask open-ended questions without getting defensive," she said. "He told me about the pressures and challenges he was facing, so I was able to feel some empathy for him."

"I'm so glad," I said.

"Beth," she said, "this was the first truly meaningful conversation I've ever had with him. It has changed my understanding of him."

It is important to note here that the NCD Process did not change their opinion of him. Rather it helped her to be able to show up for the meeting in a way that left her feeling good about herself while understanding him a little bit better.

The process can work for personal situations too.

Another client had to have a conversation with her mother-in-law. It had been weighing heavily on her mind. She'd been paying her mother-in-law for childcare for a few years. She was certain that her mother-in-law depended on this income. Her twin daughters were now old enough to go to preschool. The benefits were that the girls would be in school with other children their age and the expense would be significantly less.

The client had been putting this conversation off for several months because she was certain her mother-in-law would react badly to the news.

"I've been trying to drop hints to her," she explained.

"Why can't you be direct?" I asked.

"I've had a great relationship with her, and I'm so afraid of damaging it if I tell her we aren't going to pay her anymore."

We worked through the NCD Process to determine where her fears were blocking her from speaking her truth. We uncovered all the assumptions she was making about how her mother-in-law may feel or act in response. At the end of working through the NCD Process, the client felt ready and able to have a dialogue that was fact-based, empathetic, and emotionally clean and clear.

A few days later she called and said "Hi, Beth. So, I had the conversation with my mother-in-law, and you know what? She said that it made total sense, and she is happy to step in to help on school vacations or if the girls are ill. She said she has been looking forward to having more time to do things that haven't been possible when she's caring for the girls full-time."

When we are open, honest, and kind with our communication, it allows others to do the same with us. When we aren't trying to manipulate or manage how another person responds or feels, we will often be pleasantly surprised when we learn the truth.

NCD helps to remove fears, assumptions, biases, and stories. These thinking errors can fuel worry, fear, and anger which interfere with clear communication. With NCD, we can turn the conversation around and focus on facts.

What conversations are you resisting?

CHAPTER 6

WHY BAD COMMUNICATION HAPPENS

*The single biggest problem with communication
is the illusion that it has taken place.*

— GEORGE BERNARD SHAW

As I began trying out new ways to communicate, I found a great deal of scientific research that supported the NCD methodology, especially in situations where I perceived the stakes were high and my emotions were tense.

I was beginning to understand that it would require the deprogramming of how I'd learned to communicate. I had to teach my brain to respond in the ways I wanted, rather than reacting out of emotion, fear, or stress. The more I practiced the NCD Process myself, the more I was able to recognize and then self-manage when I felt the desire to defend, justify, lash out, or disappear when conversations got tough.

I've always been a strong and persuasive communicator. Like many strong communicators, I had been using my strengths to manipulate others to agree with me, give me what I wanted, or "win" a conflict. What I hadn't realized was that using communication skills to "win" often destroys trust and damages relationships. People tend to avoid people who they feel have power over them. While I had many people who did what I said, I didn't have the kinds of collaborative, trusting, authentic relationships I wanted.

The more I practiced the NCD Process, the more I engaged with curiosity and was open to outcomes instead of controlling them. I felt more in control of my own emotional reactions. I was able to be present in times of vulnerability, stress, or conflict with less angst.

We must stay alert for when our fears, assumptions, and thinking errors are causing us to resist challenging conversations. It takes deliberate practice to rewire what drives us to act on our brain's need for protection and control.

A defining moment for me, when I understood the impact of my fears and desires for self-protection, happened when my daughter Annie was planning her wedding.

The time leading up to a wedding can be high-stakes and emotionally intense, filled with drama and unhealthy conflict. I had been imagining that going shopping for her wedding dress would be just her, me, and her sister.

She called to tell me that her stepmom, stepsister, and mother-in-law would be coming as well. I'm embarrassed to even share my reaction with you.

"Hi, Mom," Annie said. "I just want to let you know that Kate, Fiona, and Patty are coming with us for dress shopping. And then we are all going to lunch after."

Before I even realized what was happening, I heard myself reacting with outrage.

"Annie, why? I'm the mother of the bride. This is a time for you and me and your sister as a family. Why are other people trying to take this away from me? I am the one who gave birth to you and raised you. This is my time!"

"Mom! Why are you acting like this?" Annie asked. "Other people want to be part of this, and I want them to go!" she responded.

I don't clearly recall the rest of the conversation. When we hung up, I went for a long walk. Walking gave me the pause I needed to let go of the emotional hotspot activated by my fears. Once I'd calmed down, I realized, "Of course she wants this to be a celebration and a fun event. This isn't about me or my importance in her life."

I was able to call her back and apologize. I have learned that when I feel myself becoming outraged, I need to pause, take some time, move my body, get oxygen flowing, and allow fear and the desire to protect myself to melt away. Then I can engage with clarity and emotional freedom.

This lesson served me well for the rest of the wedding planning process. I wasn't someone who caused drama and chaos. Instead, I was a supportive and loving mother.

As we learn to discern the truth behind our thoughts and emotions, we will avoid being driven by fears or a desire for self-protection and instead show up as the person we most want to be.

CHAPTER 7

SELF-PROTECTION AND THE AMYGDALA

"For there is always light.
If only we're brave enough to see it.
If only we're brave enough to be it.

— AMANDA GORMAN

THE PART OF THE BRAIN that interprets danger is called the *amygdala*. The amygdala is located near the base of the brain. It is the integrative center for emotions, emotional behavior, and motivation. It is charged with making emotional meaning from memories, desire for rewards, and the decisions you need to make. Our amygdala evaluates the emotional importance of incoming stimuli and generates a response. Since it is responsible for regulating aggression and fear, when the amygdala interprets a threat, it is quick to respond.

As human beings, we are hardwired with an automatic, self-preservation reaction to incoming stimuli that the amygdala interprets as unsafe—either physically or psychologically. This is what happened to me when my daughter shared that she was inviting others to the dress shopping event. As silly as it sounds, at that moment, my brain was interpreting this information as a threat to my importance as the mother of the bride.

When faced with a threat, the amygdala organizes a reaction known as fight or flight. This reaction has helped our species survive. Historically, this very real fight or flight reaction kept us safe from physical threats.

Now, it's more common for us to face psychological threats, situations, and events that make us feel emotionally unsafe. These can be threats to ego, the ability to make a living, fear of what others think of us, fear of failure, or threats to our values and beliefs. Or, as in my case, to the sense of my own status.

The amygdala interprets experiences based on thoughts and feelings which most often come from past experiences, fears about what may happen in the future, or insecurity about decisions we're weighing and what the outcomes might be.

These threats can be very subtle and hard to discern, especially without practice. And, to an outside observer, the threat may be completely invisible.

In NCD, reactions to psychological threats are called emotional hotspots and they can become activated at lightning speed. One moment, we are engaged in a calm, simple conversation such as the one I had with my daughter. And in the next moment, we are trying to protect ourselves from something someone else said.

Emotional hotspots can also activate as our mind replays conversations or situations that have already occurred or are expected to occur.

When an emotional hotspot is activated, it requires intentionality, practice, and some specific tools to put it on pause. Developing self-awareness enables us to recognize what is happening, intentionally pause, and then choose how to respond.

If the emotional hotspot is not disrupted, the amygdala drives what happens next. This is when communication goes off track and we say things or take actions that are likely to result in shame, guilt, and unhealthy conflict.

Conversations about money can often cause emotional hotspots to activate, both in business and personal life. Money carries a lot of emotional meaning and is also tied to our sense of security and safety. In the work world, there are many opportunities for emotional hotspots to become activated around money. When having a conversation about sales projections and revenue, it is easy for people to become defensive, angry, or even avoid the conversation.

During a conflict, when reacting to an activated emotional hotspot, we can become red in the face and try to blame other people or other circumstances. Often, any trust that has been created is destroyed. We must all learn how to manage our emotional hotspots so we can have the conversations that are necessary while maintaining our connection and positive relationships with each other.

As much as I wish that the NCD Process could be a tool for every situation and circumstance, it is not. The exceptions are:

- If the person we need to have a conversation with is living with a mental health diagnosis or a cognitive limitation.

- If the conversation is about something that puts us, the person, or others at immediate mental or physical risk.

In those cases, speak with a licensed or certified professional with expertise in that specific area.

CHAPTER 8

DISRUPTING THE AMYGDALA REACTION

*When you learn something new,
the wiring in your brain changes.*

— JOHN MEDINA, *BRAIN RULES*

THE FIRST STEP in having a drama-free dialogue is to become aware of and responsible for our own emotional energy. In NCD language, we refer to this as being aware of the energy we bring to the room.

When our amygdala perceives we are at risk, it sends a message to our adrenal gland, which, in turn, releases adrenaline and cortisol. Adrenaline prepares our body to spring into action. Cortisol acts as an alarm system and works with our brain to control mood, motivation, and fear. This alarm manifests in physical symptoms.

One way to increase awareness of our own emotional energy is to start paying attention to the physical symptoms we experience in our bodies whenever we feel vulnerable or at risk. Everyone's reaction is different. Our physical feelings and emotions will not necessarily be the same as someone else's.

Felix shared with me that he tends to be controlling and exacting in how he likes to see things done at work. This sabotages his relationship with colleagues and his boss. His boss strives for a work culture where people learn from their mistakes and follow their curiosity to create new processes, systems, and products. Although Felix intellectually understands the value of this work culture, his innate desire for control keeps him hyper-aware of how those around him are deviating from what he believes is the "right way" to do things.

"I don't even try to watch how people are doing things, but this is a small space," Felix said. "I see everything. I know it's not my job to correct people, but I can't seem to help it. And the feedback I get is that when I do correct people, it comes out in ways that cause them to be offended. I don't want that to be the case. I just want people to do things right

"Beth, I know I must learn to manage this behavior. How can I do that?" he asked in our session.

Awareness and a desire to make a shift are the first steps. If someone isn't open to change, there isn't much a coaching session can do to help. Felix clearly indicated he saw the need and had the desire to change. Now, he just needed the tools.

A primary driver of Felix's inability to resist this behavior is that he felt he must protect what he believed to be the right way to do things. When he saw things happening outside what he valued as the right way, his amygdala went into overdrive trying to protect that.

"Felix, close your eyes for a minute, and think back to a time when you jumped in and told someone they were doing something wrong," I said. "What did you feel in your body?"

My intention was to get him out of his thoughts and into the physical sensations created when adrenaline and cortisol started pulsing through his system.

"My shoulders tensed up. My hands got tight and sweaty. I felt my jaw tightening," he responded.

"Do you recognize these physical sensations as familiar?"

He responded without hesitation. "Oh, yes. I sure do."

Felix had become aware of what it felt like in his physical body when experiencing an emotional hotspot. Now, he can pause, breathe, calm the hotspot, and determine how he wants to proceed rather than react in a way that he doesn't want to.

This process requires practice. Felix will likely forget sometimes and react to his colleagues in ways that have the potential to damage relationships. But in those moments, he can stop and apologize rather than experience shame and guilt later. In time, his practice will pay off and his new habit will become pausing, assessing, and then proceeding.

Because Felix is the most experienced person in the room, there may be times when safety or the integrity of the product is truly at stake. In those rare instances, Felix will pause long enough to assess the level of risk at hand and then make a very intentional decision to intervene.

The most common physical sensations caused by the release of adrenaline and cortisol are sweaty palms, racing heart, flushed skin, and butterflies in the stomach. One woman I worked with said that her early warning was an old wrist injury that would flare up and throb. Another person stated that they got a strange sensation in their toes. Personally, I feel my shoulders hunch forward. I am compelled to brace myself by tightening the muscles in my face and neck. I feel heat rising from my chest and into my neck.

It doesn't matter what or where we feel the warning signals of an emotional hotspot. What matters is that we gain familiarity with what sensations we experience every time we feel at risk. The more we pay attention to our body, the more we will be able to recognize when we're headed for a fight or flight reaction.

Most of the time, when we are experiencing an activated emotional hotspot, it isn't visible to others around us. But they will notice the actions we take as a result.

Think about the thought bubbles over a character's head in a cartoon. The thought bubble doesn't represent the words that are being spoken. Thought bubbles indicate what is going on inside the mind of the character, and that is not transparent to anyone around them.

We all walk around with thought bubbles. You likely have a thought bubble happening right now. It is full of your assumptions, unspoken expectations, questions that you have, emotions lingering from past experiences, and fears of the future. All these thoughts are informed by any biases you may hold.

When we act on the contents of our thought bubble, it can confuse others because they don't have insight into our thoughts.

In NCD, we call the contents of the thought bubbles "stories." Stories are what generate the emotional energy behind the words we speak or the actions we take. When we are experiencing an emotional hotspot, our words and actions can become exaggerated and confusing to others.

In my story meeting with an influential businessman, I was on the verge of giving his assistant a piece of my mind. I wanted to be sure that she, Robert, and I were all clear that I was right, and she was wrong. My amygdala's desire to protect my ego by proving I was right was overriding my desire for connection. My exaggerated reaction to this mistake would have been confusing to both the assistant and Robert and would have likely sabotaged me from achieving the meeting I wanted so badly.

When our amygdala is driving our reaction, it is hard to avoid the desire to protect ourselves. Facts become buried under the fight or flight response. In NCD, we refer to fight tendencies as "expanding" behaviors and flight tendencies as "shrinking" behaviors.

Becoming aware of our individual tendency to either shrink or expand helps us to be proactive in recognizing and disrupting amygdala reactions. When we're able to interrupt the desire to shrink or expand, we can be intentional in the actions we choose and the words we speak as successful communicators.

CHAPTER 9

HEALTHY CONFLICT IS NECESSARY

*You don't need to find your voice.
You just need to use it.*

— PATTI DIGH

CONFLICT GROWS out of the tension that exists when two or more people bring their own perspectives to a conversation. Conflict is a necessary part of creativity, innovation, forward movement, and problem-solving. Whenever two humans come together, be it to form a relationship or to solve a challenge, conflict will be present.

Whether this conflict is healthy, unhealthy, good, bad, productive, or unproductive is up to us. The power to transform conflict from unhealthy to healthy lies in our self-awareness, emotional self-management, willingness to be curious, and our commitment to focus on the good of the whole rather than our individual gains.

Healthy conflict helps us to know each other better, experience empathy, and build trust. Through the perseverance of working through hard things together, we can solve even the most difficult challenges. In healthy conflict, no individual wins or loses. Instead, the outcome makes things better for the collective.

Unhealthy conflict damages relationships by forcing one person to sacrifice so the other person is the victor. In unhealthy conflict, conscious or not, one person is intending to hurt or weaken the position of the other. Often in unhealthy conflict people feel attacked and things are taken personally.

When conflict makes an abrupt shift from healthy to unhealthy, it is most often because one or more parties suddenly feel the need to protect their ego. Although we can't control how others show up in conflict, we can choose to be curious about what our ego is protecting and how we respond.

Cara told me that her teenage daughter was really starting to exercise her independence.

"I've been frustrated lately because Christina is questioning my authority and pushing back on my decisions on just about everything," Cara said in our consultation. "We get into huge arguments. Yesterday she asked if she could come home an hour later than usual. I said, 'No. The rule is that you are to be home by 11:00 p.m.' She asked why, and I heard myself saying what I said I'd never say, 'Because I said so.' I always despised it when my own mother used that phrase. And now, here I am using it with my own daughter. And she reacted exactly as I did. She stormed off and hasn't spoken to me since. I feel like I'm not only losing control of my daughter but also losing my relationship with her."

"I have a question for you, Cara," I said. "What is it, aside from your daughter, that you are trying to protect by saying no?"

Cara sat back and thought for a while and responded, "I don't want to lose control over her."

"Say more about that," I said.

"If I lose control of her, how will she stay safe? The world is crazy. The later she is out of the house, the bigger chance there is something that could go badly. Waiting for her to get home and worrying is so exhausting. She doesn't understand how vulnerable she is," Cara told me. She was clearly concerned, and her face showed it.

"Do you remember back when your own mother used the phrase, 'Because I said so.'? How did that make you feel?" I inquired, hoping to tap into her empathy for her younger self.

"I felt like she didn't believe that I was responsible or smart enough to make good decisions. That I was still a child instead of someone who was growing up."

I paused to let that sink in a little.

Cara continued, "I guess Christina feels the same way, right? I mean, she does make good choices. She is very responsible. I'm just so afraid of something happening to her. The world is so unpredictable right now. And she is growing up so fast. She will be going off to college or to start her own life in just a few years. I feel like every single day she is less interested in spending time with me and more focused on building her own life. It makes me sad."

"What do you want to protect by saying 'no'?" I asked, repeating my earlier inquiry.

"The time I have left with her as a little girl and me as her mother—I'm so afraid that is vanishing," she responded sadly.

"Do you know why Christina wants to stay out for the extra hour? Have you asked her why that's important to her?"

"No. Not really. I just assume that's what kids want. To keep pushing the boundaries," she answered

"Maybe it is time that you actually engaged with curiosity," I said. "Find out why it matters to her. Let her know why you are resistant. And then inquire what strategies she has for keeping herself safe. Let her know that what you really want is to feel connected to her even though you know she is growing up and becoming more independent. And for her to be safe. How would it feel to have that kind of discussion?"

Cara sighed with relief. "That kind of discussion feels more appropriate given that she is growing up, and our relationship is shifting. It would feel like relating in a new way."

"You still can say no," I reminded her. "But you will do it from a more informed place. You and she may even be able to co-create a solution that serves both of you better. I'm interested to hear how it goes."

Cara reported back to me that she and her daughter were now communicating better. Based on Christina's responses to Cara's inquiries about how she would make decisions about safety and responsibility, Cara was feeling more relieved. Cara said that when she let go of being the controller and engaged with genuine curiosity, the conversations they were having were some of the best moments they'd had in a long time.

How we engage in conflict and tough conversations determines how our relationships evolve. Shifting from unhealthy conflict into healthy conflict can transform relationships, so they grow and develop as our roles shift.

When you are seen as the person responsible for the emotional safety of a group or team, and you let unhealthy conflict fester, then morale, teamwork, and camaraderie will be negatively impacted.

I was working with a supervisor who told me that he had a challenge with two valued contributors on his team, John and Lucille. These co-workers refused to speak to each other even though they were on the same team, in the same office.

"The situation is not impacting the quality of their individual contributions. But when it comes to group projects, it is a nightmare. And things are becoming more and more uncomfortable for everyone around them," he said, exasperated.

"Tell me what is happening when you perceive others are uncomfortable?" I asked.

"Well, when we have meetings, Lucille, who is normally a strong contributor, shuts down if John is there. I can't get her to speak. And John makes negative comments that I assume are referencing the situation between him and Lucille, but they are vague enough that I don't know how to handle them," he said. "I'm afraid if I call him out, it will make matters worse."

"Was it always this way?" I asked, curious to find out more.

"Oh, no," he quickly replied. "They started as great collaborators. Then, as a company, we had some financial setbacks and had to cut back on staffing. We had to cut a position from the department."

He went on to say, "I asked all the managers for feedback on which position to cut. Most of the managers were able to look at the big picture. One option was to cut John's administrator, who everyone liked, but didn't have a heavy workload."

"Lucille also had a position on her team that we considered, and that stressed her out," he said. "I was taken aback by how angry she became. She campaigned strongly for retaining her person. Maybe a little too strongly and not always appropriately."

Shaking his head he said, "I could tell she was threatened by the thought of losing this person, but she also wasn't wrong. I made the decision that John's administrator would be the position to be cut. I suspect that John blames Lucille instead of understanding that it was a decision made in the best interest of the department. I still don't think he sees that. Ever since then it seems he has a grudge against Lucille. And she won't even speak to him."

"I've tried talking to them individually, but I don't like conflict. I just want everyone to be happy," he continued. "What I've been doing is just avoiding having them work together at all. This isn't always easy because we are a small team, and we rely on each other."

Most of us aren't taught to recognize or lead through unhealthy conflict. This is a clear example of a leader who doesn't yet have this necessary skill. The result is that relationships are damaged, grudges fester, and everyone in proximity suffers.

When I started this journey, I did not understand that not everyone is comfortable with conflict. I grew up with two parents who could argue vehemently over business decisions and strategies and then ten minutes later, my dad would come up behind my mother washing the dishes and give her a big hug. It was never personal for them. I grew up understanding that I could argue and disagree about how to get something done, but it wasn't personal.

Every relationship carries the possibility of igniting emotional hotspots within us. Unmanaged, emotional hotspots can quickly lead to defensiveness, blaming, and anger.

As an outside observer, it is difficult to discern the difference between healthy and unhealthy conflict. Both can be heated, passionate, and uncomfortable. However, the difference between the two is that in unhealthy conflict, the goal is to win or dominate. When we become attached to proving that our way of thinking is right or justified, there is no opportunity for curiosity, growth, or learning. Relationships quickly become damaged.

During unhealthy conflict, emotional hotspots are activated and the parts of your brain responsible for empathy, collaboration, and the good of the whole are shut down. All the focus goes toward self-protection with fight or flight.

Consider when two people are engaged in a physical fight. They do not pause and inquire how the other is feeling or tell them they value their relationship. Often, by the end of such a fight, adrenaline is so high that neither really recalls what exactly started the fight in the first place.

To be a steward of healthy conflict, show up with curiosity and wonder. Do this by asking questions that have no right or wrong answer. Curiosity allows for perspective on how they see the issue, what is important to them, and how they came to believe what they do.

Raul, an executive at a large company, has one director under him who often expresses feeling marginalized and left out of important meetings.

"I'm so tired of her continually asking to be a part of these meetings. I keep telling her that given all that is on her plate, some meetings are just not a good use of her time," he told me in a recent coaching session. "I know she's really mad about being excluded. I keep hearing from others that she is venting about it. It is starting to affect our working relationship."

"Do you know why she wants to attend the meetings?" I inquired.

"Well, I'm assuming she just wants to have her nose in everything. And it's not necessary," he answered rather defensively,

"I'm wondering what you might learn if you simply asked her instead of assuming that you know," I responded, encouraging him to use curiosity.

He begrudgingly agreed to ask her why she wanted to be included in the meetings, even though he was convinced that it was not a good use of her time.

In the next session, he told me, "I'm glad I asked. She explained that even though her position doesn't make her a decision-maker in the specific processes we are talking about, listening and understanding the context and timing of decisions being made gives her what she needs to better prepare her staff for when the new products are ready for distribution. She can begin working on the training materials they need so everything rolls out more smoothly and effectively. It actually made a lot of sense, and I was not looking at it from that perspective."

When Raul was able to let go of being the expert in this situation and engage with curiosity, he was able to find a resolution. In this case, the director attending the meeting did serve the good of the whole.

When you engage in healthy conflict, do so with the understanding that through the friction, a solution is developed that has the potential to be even stronger or more creative than you alone could come up with.

In healthy conflict, be courageous enough to pause and inquire when someone seems defensive or stuck in their position.

Even if someone isn't committed to shifting unhealthy conflict to healthy conflict, you can choose how you are going to show up. Committing to engaging with conflict in healthy ways will not only feel better, but it will reduce the amount of residual drama and stress.

CHAPTER 10

ANGER PLAYS A ROLE IN SELF-COACHING

Anger is not a pure emotion. It is made up of secondary emotions like fear and sadness that can be very uncomfortable to acknowledge.

— BETH WONSON

WHEN LOOKING AT THE ROLE of anger through the NCD lens, you'll find that anger is often not a pure emotion. Anger is usually either a manifestation of fear, sadness, or a combination of the two.

The emotions that humans least like to experience and most often try to avoid are fear, grief, anxiety, and sadness. Masking these with anger is a way to avoid the discomfort of difficult feelings.

The benefit of anger is that it often spurs us to act to right wrongs or fix what we aren't happy with. That can be a very good thing. However, when anger motivates us to act impulsively, without intention, it can result in unnecessary drama, chaos, and unhealthy conflict.

Use anger as a signal to ask self-coaching questions such as, "What am I sad about?" or "What am I fearful of losing or experiencing?" This can help uncover what is being masked by the anger so you can deal with it appropriately.

Camila shared this with me in a coaching session:

"I was tense and on edge throughout the whole weekend we were away. I was snappy with my kids. I admit that. But a few days after I got home, a friend who wasn't on the trip told me that one of my friends was calling others to say they were concerned with my parenting skills. She said that I was out of control. I was so angry! I wanted to call her up and tell her we are done as friends. How could she do this?"

"Say more," I encouraged her.

"I'm so angry. First of all, my kids are older than hers. And yes, they were being disrespectful and behaving badly. I felt embarrassed. Secondly, I was exhausted. The pressure from work is doing me in. Taking a weekend to spend time with them was important to me, but I really couldn't afford to not work that weekend. Two of my friends are stay-at-home moms. And the other doesn't even have children. I felt like they had no idea what I'm dealing with and that we have less and less in common. But we've been friends for so long, I don't want to let it go."

I asked Camila about her anger.

On a scale of 1 to 5, how angry was she? She indicated that she was "at about a six." She said that the anger she was feeling was interrupting her sleep and distracting her during the day. "I just have to tell her how mad I am, so I can get over it."

This last statement is the indication that anger was leading Camila to act.

By following the NCD Process, Camila was able to pause and delve into the emotions that were under the anger. Camila revealed that she was sad that she could not shake the stress of her business enough to truly enjoy the time with her friends and family. When asked what she was fearing, she revealed that because of their differing lifestyles and priorities, these group vacations were not as much fun as in the "old days." She was afraid of what that might mean. Was this the end of an era? What will their friendships look like moving forward? She was afraid of the loss.

As we talked, Camila became aware that the conversation she thought she wanted to have, one about how angry she was with her friend, wasn't the conversation she needed to have. Instead, she determined that she wanted to look at managing her own stress. Then she could decide what made sense for her in terms of connecting with this group given that they are all in different places in their lives.

When I asked Camila how she felt turning the conversation around compared to how she felt when we started out, she expressed that the anger had lifted. Now she felt curious and hopeful. She left the conversation eager to chat with her friend about their lives and their connection and how they could move forward in ways that supported them both.

PART III

THE PRINCIPLES

OF NCD

CHAPTER 11

BE AWARE OF THE ENERGY YOU BRING TO THE ROOM

Your emotions determine the power that your words carry.

— BETH WONSON

HAVE YOU EVER been enjoying a great day where everything is aligning for you? You are feeling chipper and bright. Then you enter a room and the person waiting for you is quite glum and grumpy. Perhaps they are venting about the recent stock market decline or sharing their negative predictions of how the new boss will impact their happiness at work. Suddenly, your mood begins to dull. You entered feeling optimistic and joyful, and you are leaving feeling down and negative.

That is because our emotions are, in a sense, contagious. As humans, we are highly sensitive to the emotions and emotional stimuli that are all around us. Sensing the emotional energy in the room is one of the ways that you can discern if you want to stay and engage or if you need to protect yourself. Each of us has different levels of ability to sense the emotional energy before responding or reacting.

Self-leadership includes checking on the emotional energy that you are bringing into your conversation. When you show up in a room with emotional baggage from whatever you were doing last, you are polluting this new experience with your leftover emotions. Showing up centered and calm sets the stage for healthy communication.

I met with Mark, an executive who is so busy that his meetings often overlap. Since his work went remote, he finds that he is really missing the time he used to take to walk from one meeting room to the next.

"Even though the time to physically move from one meeting to the next wasn't scheduled and often caused me to be late, it gave me a few minutes to shake off the emotional energy from the last meeting, take a breath, and walk into the next meeting with a fresh outlook," he told me.

"Now I don't have to even stand up. I simply click a button and move from one online meeting room to the next. I haven't even had a second to stretch my legs, take a breath, or put the last meeting behind me."

I listened to him and wondered aloud, "How does that impact the people in the next meeting?"

"I hadn't thought about that," Mark responded. "But now that I'm thinking about it, I'm sure if it was a tough meeting, I'm bringing angst, stress, and frustration with me. And they are probably wondering why I'm showing up that way."

Energetically, the person with the most power or status, formal or informal, is the one whose energy sets the tone for the interaction. In many meetings he attends, Mark is the person with the most status, so the energy he enters with has a significant impact on how the others show up and participate.

It is tempting to try and take care of the emotions of others but that can wear you down. I work with so many people who talk about being emotionally burnt out. When this is the case,

I check in to see how much of other people's emotional work the person is trying to do.

My recommendation to Mark was to schedule meetings to end ten minutes before the next one starts. This isn't always possible because most of his meetings aren't scheduled by him.

Here's a practice for calming the energy you bring to each engagement:

- Notice the energy you are feeling.

- Close your eyes and breathe in through your nose and out through your mouth.

- Listen for the beat of your heart and express gratitude for it.

- Notice where in your body you feel any tension or discomfort and release it on the out-breath.

- Repeat 3 to 4 times.

- Remind yourself of the purpose of your next interaction (What are the facts here and now?).

- Open your eyes and show up fresh and emotionally centered for the next interaction.

The only person you can manage is yourself. This includes being accountable for your own emotional energy.

CHAPTER 12

THE ONLY PERSON I CAN MANAGE IS MYSELF

The happiness of others is not your responsibility.

— BETH WONSON

WHEN SOMEONE REVEALS to me that they feel burnt out, I check to see just how much work they are doing to make sure others are happy. What I usually discover is that they are operating under the belief that it is their job to make others happy. It's not. We are each responsible for our own happiness. We can create joyful moments for others through gifts, surprises, or pleasing behaviors. However, true happiness comes from within.

Trying to manage another person into happiness leads to exhausting yourself physically and mentally. Indicators that you are trying to lead others to happiness include resisting speaking your truth, avoiding giving feedback, not setting boundaries, or not being clear about expectations. As tempting as avoidance behaviors may be, they will never lead to satisfying long-term results.

When managers come to me because they are burnt out and overwhelmed, I always listen for references to "employee happiness." Callie, a seasoned manager in a social service agency, told me that she was burnt out. She was feeling more pressure now that it was harder to hire and retain quality employees.

"I really do everything I can to make people happy at work. I plan events such as potlucks and pizza parties. We instituted dress-down days where everyone can wear jeans or yoga pants to work. I bring donuts every Friday. And more than anything else, I avoid giving critical feedback. I can't risk making someone unhappy and having them leave. And yet, I feel like everything I'm doing is having no impact. I'm exhausted," Callie explained.

Here's what Callie doesn't understand.

As a manager, it's your job to make sure that your employees are engaged in work that uses their unique strengths, talents, and experience in ways that are purposeful and support the goals of the organization. It's the manager's responsibility to point out performance gaps with clarity and kindness while empowering employees to close those gaps. A manager ensures that the work environment is emotionally and physically safe and employees are compensated appropriately for their contributions.

When people are seen, heard, and empowered to use their skills and talents, they are often satisfied with their work. Satisfaction may lead to happiness. An employee's happiness, however, is their own responsibility, not yours.

A principle of NCD is the belief that people are capable of managing their own happiness. When they are not happy, they need to find tools such as therapy, coaching, or medical support to identify what is wrong and make changes.

Having a challenging dialogue with someone may result in them reacting with tears, frustration, or anger. Managing those feelings is up to them, not you. When you try to create an environment where people don't have to manage their own emotions, you are trying to do their emotional work for them, and that's impossible. This is where exhaustion and burnout form.

Don't lose the focus of the dialogue you want to have by trying to stop a reaction. Pause and be curious. Tears, for example, have a multitude of possible meanings. You have no way of knowing exactly what the tears are about or why the tears are happening. They are a very natural bodily function just like hair growing on someone's head. You wouldn't put your hand on someone's head and say, "Oh, please. There, there. There's no need for that hair to grow."

I always recommend that you have a box of tissues handy and visible for in-person conversations. Just trust the other person to take one if needed. Don't act on someone else's tears based on what you are making the tears mean. You can, if you feel it is appropriate, pause and become curious. "I see tears. Can you tell me what they mean?"

Personally, I cry when I'm happy. I cry when I see someone being recognized for doing something good. I cry when I'm experiencing stress relief. And I cry when I'm angry.

By operating under the premise that each person has the capability, tools, and resources to manage their own happiness, you are seeing them as a whole and fully empowered human. That, in and of itself, is empowering to others.

CHAPTER 13

GRACE IS IN THE SPACE

Almost everything will work again if you unplug it for a few minutes, including you.

— ANNE LAMOTT

BEFORE DEVELOPING NCD, when I was going through a very difficult time, I would find myself spiraling into fear of the future. My mind would go down a rabbit hole of "what if" which would prompt me to take unproductive actions and lash out in anger.

I needed a tool to help manage my mind's desire to go down this unhealthy path. I created a list of ten things that I knew would immediately bring me back to a centered calm.

I posted this list on my nightstand, my bedroom mirror, the dashboard of my car, on my computer, and on the front of my planner.

Anytime I noticed I had begun to descend into these fear-filled thoughts, I would just run my finger down the list and do whatever activity it landed on. I made sure the things on my list were accessible, simple, and easy to do so that I could shift to them quickly.

I created this strategy out of desperation. I was so tired of getting stuck in my fears and worrying about things I had no control over. I wanted to move out of this space and start living my life in a healthier way.

Here's what my list looked like:
- Breathe
- Look at the ocean
- Go into the garden
- Eat healthy food
- Sleep
- Go for a walk outside
- Play with my dog
- Meditate
- Spend time with my horse
- Write

What I didn't realize at the time was that I was retraining myself to notice what was happening, to pause and stop the spiral, and then engage with what was real and true at this moment. It kept me from wallowing in fear and unknowns.

I started calling this practice, *Putting Grace in the Space*. By putting *Grace* in the *Space*, you recognize the automatic reaction that is happening inside you and choose to disrupt the emotional hotspot activation. It's a principle of NCD. *Space* refers to the time between when you feel as if an emotional hotspot has been activated and when you choose to respond to the situation. *Grace* refers to intentionally giving yourself permission to breathe, shift from your thoughts to the facts, and use the NCD Process.

When you are experiencing an emotional hotspot, a good remedy is to bring oxygen into your system in an intentional way. Breathing in through your nose, allowing the air to go deep into your chest, and then releasing it through your mouth provides exactly the amount of oxygen that your body can process at one time. Gulping air through your mouth floods your lungs with more oxygen than it can process and may cause the amygdala to become even more concerned that you are at risk.

When your amygdala sends a signal to your adrenal glands that you need to protect yourself, those glands pump hormones into your bloodstream. These hormones tell your bloodstream to send the majority of the oxygen-rich blood to the parts of your brain responsible for shrinking or expanding reactions. Less oxygen-rich blood is sent to the parts of your brain responsible for curiosity, empathy, collaboration, problem-solving, and innovation. This whole process happens on your behalf with you barely being aware of it.

There may be some physical warning signals such as sweaty palms, accelerated heart rate, fluttering in your chest, or flushed skin. The exact nature of these warning signals, indicating an emotional hotspot is being activated, varies from person to person. You are probably more familiar with what your warning signals feel like than you realize because we each seem to experience the same ones again and again. If you don't become familiar with what the early warning signals feel like to you, you miss the opportunity to disrupt the process. And before you know it, you are on the pathway to either expanding your presence to verbally attack or defend yourself, or you are figuring out how to get the heck out of there.

Putting Grace in the Space is the conscious act of noticing your personal warning signs when an emotional hotspot is activated. Take a deep breath through your nose and into your lungs and exhale through your mouth while grounding your feet on the floor. This alleviates the physical symptoms and brings your awareness out of your mind and into your body to calm the fight or flight response. You can return to a centered and balanced emotional energy. At the same time, listen for the beat of your heart and express gratitude for all your heart does to support you and pump that oxygen-rich blood through your system. This calms your mind and allows you to come back to a balanced state.

It is within this balanced and centered space that you look at the true facts of a situation and decide how you want to deliberately proceed.

I practice this every day. I put grace in the space while I'm transitioning from one meeting to the next or if I'm in a conversation and feel myself getting anxious or stressed. It only takes a few seconds and is invisible to anyone else.

CHAPTER 14

THAT'S FASCINATING

*If you want to win a tug of war,
simply let go of the rope.*

— UNKNOWN

WE'VE BEEN SOCIALIZED to believe that it is important to prove our own expert status by having something to say in response to everything that is said to us. When operating in expert mode, real dialogue is nearly impossible.

Real dialogue occurs when two or more people are sharing their perspective, being curious about others' perspectives, listening deeply, and developing empathy and understanding. In real dialogue, there are no winners and losers. In real dialogue, all parties feel seen, heard, and validated—even when there isn't agreement.

In my example of a direct report who felt marginalized, the manager, Raul, began to engage with more curiosity instead of readying an answer to every request. In turn, the direct report began to feel more seen and heard. It doesn't mean that Raul agreed with her in every instance, but he was able to stop bracing himself against her constant need for validation. Together they co-created solutions that resulted in improvements, and she felt more respected and engaged.

There will be times when you are a curious learner, while the other party is committed to being in expert mode. That's okay. Remain curious and use your tools to help them begin to let go of expert mode by validating and acknowledging them.

There will be times, particularly when dialogue is stressful, when it is critical to validate that you have heard the other person, even when you don't agree. In these situations, I find myself saying, "That's fascinating."

It's a simple and effective response when you don't have an answer or an opinion to share. It gives you space to absorb what you're hearing and lets the other person know you've heard them.

I learned a lot about letting go of expert status from my daughters. When they were becoming young adults, they would tell me things they planned to do or things they believed to be true. I would often feel the need to show my expertise. I would set them straight, give them advice, or tell them what wouldn't work out. This caused a lot of unhealthy conflict between us. They became frustrated when I shot down their ideas instead of having a dialogue with them.

Every time they had a new idea, I would feel anxious and believe that it was my responsibility to tell them all the pros and cons. I believed that I was protecting them.

One day I just started saying, "That's fascinating. Tell me more." To my delight, they would.

This presented an opportunity for dialogue. This approach dramatically reduced the amount of energy I had to expend. I learned more about what they were thinking. Most of the time, whatever idea they had morphed or fizzled out just by talking it through. Our connection grew stronger.

Miles told me that he had two directors who, because of their areas of responsibility, were frequently in conflict. One of the two would ask him to step in and resolve the issue. The other director indicated she felt that she was at a disadvantage because Miles frequently sided with the first director. Throughout the company, Miles was getting a reputation for favoring one director over the other.

In our coaching, we talked about being "the expert."

"How does it feel to always be the one who has the solution when these two directors are in disagreement?" I asked Miles.

"It is so much quicker to just break the tie. I usually side with Andrea. She and I think alike. She has more experience with the company. It just so happens that she is always the one who bumps it up to me. My fear is that she then goes back to Lisa saying, 'Miles agrees with me,' and I guess, now that I think about it, that isn't great," he answered.

"I'm curious. Why not empower them to resolve the conflict themselves?"

Miles was taken aback, "I've never thought of that. You mean to give it back to them?"

"Yes. It sounds like they are competent. And they understand the goals of the task. Is that right?"

"Yes. That's right. But I have no idea how to do that. I just automatically make the decision."

"You tell me that you are constantly interrupted by your direct reports to make decisions and referee conflicts and this leaves you exhausted as well as sucks up your time. Did I hear that correctly?"

"You did," he answered, as his cell phone pinged with new texts dropping in.

"Respond right now to Andrea and say, 'That's an interesting challenge. Revisit the goals of the task together, and then let me know how you two resolve it.'"

Miles lightened and smiled. "Really? I can do that?"

"Not only can you do that, you should do it. Your job is to empower your reports to use their skills and talents to resolve conflicts. The key is to remind them of the goals of the task as well as any expectations you have. This is a great time-saving practice for you and builds the relationship between them."

It's hard to break the pattern of being the expert because every time you can answer a question for someone or solve their problem, you receive a reward in the form of a dopamine hit in your brain. Our brains come to crave dopamine and can predict what will generate the reward. That's why we like being able to answer questions quickly, resolve conflicts, and remove people from discomfort.

Most of us have been socialized to have all the answers. As a small child, you were likely asked to perform and demonstrate what you know. "Show Grandma how you can count to ten." or "Say your A, B, Cs, honey." When you enter school, everything is about performing and demonstrating the knowledge you have. In the work world, promotions, raises, and even getting a job in the first place are based on how well you perform by demonstrating your skills and knowledge.

But when it comes to building relationships, increasing empathy, and helping others feel seen and heard, it is important to give the expert mode a rest.

The next time you feel yourself getting ready to be the expert while someone is talking to you, shift to being fascinated. Pause, listen, ask curious questions, and repeat. The people around you will feel empowered and validated.

CHAPTER 15

CURIOSITY IS THE PATHWAY TO EMPATHY

People are motivated and empowered by sharing their ideas and knowledge. They just need a bit of prompting.

— BETH WONSON

CURIOSITY IS A CORNERSTONE of the NCD Process. Being curious about your reactions builds self-awareness. Being curious about others cultivates empathy, and empathy builds trust. Choosing to be fascinated instead of being an opinionated expert is the first step in using curiosity as a tool.

More than ever, people are passionately arguing for and defending their positions, opinions, and beliefs, especially in public forums like social media. Perhaps you've found yourself in a kerfuffle or two. I know I have. Someone posts something that goes against my beliefs or values and suddenly an emotional hotspot is activated in me. Instantly, I feel my chest and shoulders tighten, my skin feels flushed, and I'm leaning toward my keyboard, fingers poised to set them straight. If I don't pause and put grace in the space, it's on. I become part of a social media thread, arguing back and forth with someone I may barely know. Eventually, it entangles a whole group of others who are only tangentially connected to me or the original author of the post. Feelings are hurt. I've "unfriended" people or they've unfriended me. I'm left with a bad feeling about it all and no real way to resolve it. Worst of all, no opinions are changed, but connections are lost, and relationships are damaged.

Once I realized how unproductive and unhealthy it is to argue on social media, I began deploying curiosity. Instead of putting on my expert hat and typing a persuasive response, I'd ask an open-ended, curious question like, "Could you say more about that?" or "Would you share how you came to that conclusion?" or "Do you have an example you could share with me?"

Curious questions asked without manipulation or the need to win, provide space in an argument or debate. In this space, both parties can pause the posturing and bracing, if only for a moment. Curiosity creates space to take a breath so that you can shift your thoughts. Best of all, you get to learn something new about their perspective. As you reflect on their response, you may also learn more about your own perspective.

When we engage with curiosity, especially when dialogue is uncomfortable, empathy begins to develop. Empathy has become a buzzword. Corporate leaders are promoting empathy as a value, business writers are publishing "how to" empathy books, and professional development providers are selling one-day empathy skill-building workshops.

But authentic empathy is not something you apply like ointment on a wound. Authentic empathy is something that is developed between people as they come to know each other, share their perspectives, and become genuinely curious about how the other person thinks and what they value. Empathy comes alive when we stick with challenging dialogues, believing that there may be something to learn, even when it is difficult and uncomfortable.

CHAPTER 16

YOU CAN ONLY SEE THE WORLD THROUGH YOUR OWN LENS

*We don't see things as they are;
we see them as we are.*

— ANAÏS NIN

THE LENS THROUGH WHICH we see the world is made up of our values, socialization, education, experiences, biases, culture and heritage, and even our communication style. Our view is unique because it is made up of things that are unique to our life experiences.

You can only see the world through your own lens. There are as many different views as there are people in the world. No view is wrong. But we can spend hours or even years arguing over whose view is right, instead of trying to understand more about each other's perspective. Communication flows when we're being curious about what's behind the opinion, belief, or position that is causing disagreement.

It may feel like your reasoning is completely obvious, but often it is not transparent to others.

I talk to my clients about decoding themselves for others. That means proactively explaining how you arrived at your position, why you feel so passionately about it, and what values or beliefs are informing it. By practicing decoding, we can be more certain what others know about our thought process, and it encourages them to do the same. Unspoken thoughts are very real components of dialogue, even when they aren't transparent.

A few years ago, I was working with a leadership team and the two owners of the company. We had three full days of work ahead of us. The first morning was about brainstorming as a group. Every time one of the participants shared an idea, one of the owners would grimace and shift in her chair. Everyone was noticing it and before long, brainstorming came to a halt. I was beginning to panic. My job was to facilitate brainstorming, and it wasn't happening.

I assumed that the owner was unhappy with the process. I became distracted while my mind raced trying to figure out how to shift what I was doing so that I could make her happy. But then I paused and became curious. I asked her directly what was happening to her at this moment.

I said, "I see your body language but I'm not sure what it means. Can you help me understand?" Then I held my breath and waited.

To my surprise, she said, "Yesterday, I had my first day off in months, and I worked in my garden for six straight hours without stopping. Every time I so much as breathe, I get a sharp pain in my back. I keep moving around to try to find a comfortable position in my chair."

There was a collective sigh of relief in the room.

In the absence of information, we conjure up stories about what other people are thinking or feeling and often put ourselves at the center of them. From my perspective, I was certain her body language was about my facilitation, and everyone else in the room was certain it was about the value of their contributions. Our stories were based on the flawed fact that her behavior was about us.

We limit what is possible in collaboration until we pause and get curious. It took courage for me to ask her directly, but it was the only possible way to clarify the truth. Staying committed to your own view of the world, without being curious, wastes time and damages trust. To improve our world, we need to open ourselves to communication.

CHAPTER 17

TRUST IS BUILT ONE CONVERSATION AT A TIME AND ONE EXPERIENCE AT A TIME

The ability to trust others begins with the confidence to trust yourself.

— BETH WONSON

WE HAVE A LACK OF UNDERSTANDING of what trust is and what it isn't. Through movies or novels, we've come to romanticize trust so much so that it can feel like trust is an all-or-nothing proposition. The reality is that our degree of trust depends on the situation.

For example, when I'm facilitating a group of clients, after just a few hours I'd trust each of them with my belongings if I were to step out of the room. However, I'm not going to trust them with my passwords to my bank account or to mail my taxes by the deadline. That may change over time as we share more conversations and experiences, but as of right now, I won't.

We begin healthy relationships with a level of trust that is appropriate for the situation and how well we know each other. Trust is built one conversation at a time and one experience at a time. And trust is destroyed in much the same way, only faster.

To have emotionally clean and clear communication, it is important that we honor that trust. Once we have a successful experience where trusting each other pays off, we are likely to trust even more in the future. As we get to know someone and understand how they've formed their lens on the world, we are likely to trust them even further, even if we don't agree.

But trust is fragile. It can be destroyed with just one falter or misstep. Trust crumbles much like an avalanche, rapidly falling away and taking the entire relationship with it. It is far easier to initially build trust than it is to rebuild trust after it has been broken. After all, our brain loves to seek evidence that our worst fears are true. Our brain tends to focus on the misstep and think, "I told ya' so. You can't trust anyone."

We do have a choice in these instances. We can either allow the mental stories to take over and decide we will never trust this person again, or we can put grace in the space and sort out the facts from the fears and assumptions.

Look at the situation from the perspective of, "At what level was the trust we built appropriate and reciprocated? Am I willing to adjust how much trust I extend without going back to ground zero?"

Follow up by having an emotionally clean and clear conversation with the person using the NCD Process. It will increase connection.

Talking about trust and how to restore and rebuild it is something we rarely ever do. It serves the good of the whole to be intentional and truthful about developing and maintaining trust.

CHAPTER 18

AT THE END OF THE DAY, EVERYONE JUST WANTS TO BE SEEN AND HEARD

*Listen less with your thinking brain
and more with your heart.*

— BETH WONSON

A FEW YEARS AGO, I worked with a large organization that held public events. Their board contacted me because customer service ratings showed that attendees did not feel their concerns were being addressed. The challenge was that the team receiving the concerns was made up of seasonal hires who did not have much authority to address issues. This frustrated both the workers and the attendees.

I knew that, in general, attendees would not expect immediate action or resolution. They just wanted their concern to be heard. For the workers, listening to concerns all day long without being able to fix them was draining.

The training I created guided the workers to listen intently and affirm the attendee with statements like, "I hear you. That sounds frustrating." We gave each worker a notebook and a pen to use as they said, "Let me jot that down." This strategy was only for complaints or concerns that did not involve physical or emotional safety or required immediate attention. Many complaints involved things like the ticket queue being too long, or the prices being too high, or there wasn't enough shade or seating.

When the workers started implementing the strategy of affirming and writing notes, most of the attendees were satisfied with that action. They felt seen and heard and could now enjoy themselves at the event.

After the event, the board reported to me that the public provided feedback that they felt the workers were more positive and helpful. The workers themselves reported that they felt better able to deal with the concerns in a satisfactory and less draining manner. Helping each person feel seen and heard also reduced the workers' feelings of being overwhelmed or helpless.

A lot of conflict may be avoided simply by turning the conversation around and using the words, "I hear you."

PART IV

THE NCD PROCESS

OVERVIEW

THE FRAMEWORK

THE NCD PROCESS is a step-by-step self-coaching framework to help you get clean and clear on your emotions, thinking errors, and assumptions before attempting a tough dialogue.

Most people find that after using this framework a few times, they automatically begin self-coaching without following the guide. I recommend referring back to this framework whenever you find yourself avoiding or worrying about a particular conversation.

The four stages—*Story, Shift, Shape,* and *Share*—are very intentional in their sequencing and their content.

By going step-by-step, reflecting on the questions, you more easily open your mind to seeing your thinking process. You will learn a great deal about the recurring patterns that shape your decisions and gain insight into how you engage in conflict, how you operate under stress, and what thinking errors you tend to rely on.

As you increase your self-awareness using the NCD Process, you will increase your social and emotional competency and strengthen your self-leadership.

Before I go forward with a demonstration, here's a quick overview of each stage.

STAGE 1 — THE STORY

Think about a conversation you are dreading. Then, capture every thought, fear, emotion, and assumption that comes to mind. Write everything down on a piece of paper without filtering or judgment or editing.

By writing the story out, you are acting to stop unproductive fretting, future tripping, and even blaming or resentment that happens when we mix story with facts.

It's human nature for emotions, beliefs, and assumptions to be mixed in with facts. This first stage is critical for revealing and examining everything that can cause unhealthy conflict and drama.

STAGE 2 — SIFTING FOR FACTS

Take an in-depth look at your story through a self-reflection and self-coaching process which is based on a series of intentionally designed questions.

These questions will help you identify the facts of the situation. You'll sift out all information posing as facts. The sifting can be very uncomfortable at first since it requires that you've been thoroughly honest with yourself in Stage 1.

Stage 2 ends with a rewrite of what your conversation is about, using only the facts that remain.

STAGE 3 — SHAPING THE DIALOGUE

Dig deeper, refining the conversation into a clean and clear, fact-based approach.

Look at each of the facts you've isolated in Stage 2 and determine a) if they are truly a fact and b) if they are relevant to the situation. It's not uncommon for beliefs to masquerade as facts, and this stage will reveal those.

It is in Stage 3 that the turnaround happens.

There are two possible outcomes from Stage 3. You may realize that this is not a conversation you need to have, so no further action is needed. Or you feel well-equipped to have this conversation without worry or fear, and you will continue to Stage 4.

STAGE 4 – SHARING WHAT YOU'VE PREPARED

In the final stage, prepare yourself to have the dialogue using what you've already learned about clean and clear communication. Following a simple checklist, take responsibility for your own emotional energy as you engage in the dialogue you want to have.

Having worked through the four stages, you can show up as you want to rather than having your old patterns take the lead. This is the place of transformation.

The more you practice the four stages, the more the NCD Process will become second nature. You will better see where your thoughts lead you into the same traps, again and again. Before you know it, you will be someone who takes the lead in navigating challenging dialogues.

HANDS-ON

PRACTICING THE NCD PROCESS

As I GO IN DEPTH AND explain each stage of the NCD Process, you will be learning how to prepare for and participate in emotionally difficult conversations.

To provide even more insight into each stage, I'll demonstrate the NCD Process using an example from an actual client whose name has been changed to Avery. By examining Avery's story, you get to practice what to look for when working through your own conversations.

At the end of each Stage, you'll be prompted to practice what you've learned using an upcoming conversation from your own life that causes you to feel anxious or resistant.

STAGE 1

START WITH THE STORY

THINK ABOUT A CONVERSATION you know you must have but are avoiding. You've likely been turning your story over in your head for days or weeks. Maybe you've been discussing it with a family member or friend over and over. The more resistant you are to having the conversation, the better it will work for this exercise.

You may be tempted to choose a previous conversation that didn't go the way you hoped. Please don't do that. While you can learn from past experiences, this activity is best suited to prepare for upcoming conversations.

Feeling hesitant to have a tough conversation is an indication that you are playing a story about it over and over in your head. It may feel like you are working out the details and planning your approach, but what you are doing is adding flawed facts and emotional energy to the story behind the conversation.

When your story is left to play on repeat unexamined, it can create emotional hotspots. When you try to engage in a challenging dialogue without getting clean and clear about your story, you set the stage for misunderstandings, unhealthy conflict, and drama.

WHERE TO BEGIN

On a separate piece of paper, handwrite the whole story surrounding the conversation you need to have. It is a well-known fact that writing things out by hand increases learning by engaging more parts of the brain than typing. I strongly encourage you to follow the guidance of handwriting out your scenario for this exercise.

Use this writing exercise as the opportunity to document all of the thoughts and emotions that keep you awake at night or interrupt your focus during the day. We want them out of your head and put onto paper.

This activity is only for your eyes. Write freely and expressively in a stream-of-consciousness style. Start with a blank sheet of paper and write down whatever comes into your mind around the conversation you wish to have. Do not judge the details of your story as you write it. Ignore your inner editor that wants to silence some of your thoughts.

As you'll see below in Avery's example story, what you'll write out in Stage 1 can be quite long. Everything gets written down—thoughts, feelings, and beliefs, regardless of how silly or insignificant they may seem. Be curious about everything from the context of the conversation to the details you want to discuss. The more specific and honest you are, the more effective this exercise will be.

You may be tempted to skip past this stage, but don't. Doing the writing will ultimately bring you freedom while helping you to move forward.

QUESTIONS TO ANSWER AS YOU WRITE YOUR STORY

When writing your story, answer these questions as best you can. If you are unsure how to answer, go with your feelings and intuition. Don't judge or evaluate your answers as right or wrong. This process is meant to disrupt your brain's natural tendency when processing situations.

- With whom do you want to have a dialogue?
- What is your story as you see this specific situation?
- What is the change you hope will occur as a result of this conversation?
- How do you think the other party may react to this dialogue?
- How might you feel or react if the tables were reversed and they were addressing you?
- What outcome do you desire for yourself as a result of having this dialogue?
- What outcome do you desire for the other party?
- What feelings, sensations, or emotions do you notice in your body when thinking about this dialogue?

HOW STAGE 1 CAN GO AWRY

Self-editing in Stage 1 may remove information that is helpful in understanding recurring patterns of thinking errors, assumptions, or flawed facts. It's recognizing those patterns that leads to sustainable improvement in communication and self-leadership.

Although the NCD Process can help to examine where past tough conversations have gone off track, the scenario that you work on must be one you'll have in the future. I've seen time and again that working on a story that has already occurred is *just not as effective*.

LET'S PRACTICE STAGE 1—AVERY'S EXAMPLE

I will use Avery's story to demonstrate how each stage of the NCD Process helps transform a challenging conversation into one that is meaningful, relevant, and gets results.

In Stage 1, I asked Avery to write down *everything* she was thinking and feeling about the conversation. I encouraged her to just free-write whatever came to mind. The result is a mix of emotions, fears, assumptions, unspoken expectations, "shoulds," biases, and irrelevant facts.

Avery wrote down every thought that was keeping her awake at night or churning through her mind when she felt angry about the situation. Some of the details have been changed for confidentiality reasons. This scenario was selected because it is a common concern with which people in both my coaching practice and the workshops struggle.

Avery's story may seem long, but you'll see that it's critical to get every one of your thoughts onto the page to get the most out of this framework.

> "I need to have a hard conversation with one of my employees about the fact that she won't get her bonus because she isn't meeting one of her key performance metrics. Every time I think about discussing this with her, I feel myself shutting down and avoiding her. When we have a check-in meeting, I plan to bring it up, but then don't follow through.
>
> "She does good work in several other areas, but this particular performance metric is tied directly to her ability to get a bonus. And she hasn't made progress toward hitting it. I put the bonus in place to attempt to motivate her to do so. Money is motivating to everyone. Right?

"Successfully meeting this performance metric is essential for our company's ability to hit big picture goals. I'm afraid we are going to have a bad quarter if she doesn't hit this goal.

"I'm really angry that she isn't holding herself accountable when I know she can do better. In fact, as of right now, it just won't be possible for her to hit the metric.

"The metrics are transparent. Therefore, the rest of the team can see that she isn't hitting her metrics. I'm so worried that if she isn't held accountable, others will think badly of me as a manager. And they will wonder why they should work hard when I can't hold anyone accountable anyway. I will end up with a big problem on my hands if everyone starts slacking and no one is achieving their goals. I could end up losing the whole business. Then what? The idea of that possibility stresses me out so much.

"This is the only area where she struggles and yet it is the most important. I know I must tell her that she isn't getting the bonus. When I do, I'm afraid that she will be so upset that she will quit. Hiring is tough right now and I've already invested so much time developing her. I know her quirks and her weaknesses. I also know her strengths. In some ways, she reminds me of me at her age. I just dread the idea of starting all over again with someone I don't know.

"On the other hand, if she does stay, I fear she will be resentful and that will cause further headaches. I had an employee in the past who became negative when I gave them critical feedback. I don't want to go through that again. I go back and forth about if I even should have the conversation. The bonus idea did not work. I've had success in the past in motivating other employees through bonuses so I assumed it would be effective with this employee as well. I'm so mad I even tried that. What if I'm not even cut out to be running this company? I'm so humiliated just thinking about that!

"I value her as part of the team, and I care about her as a person. I haven't told her, but my vision is to eventually promote her to be a leader in the company, but how am I supposed to do that when she isn't even trying to hit the benchmarks? I lay awake at night trying to figure out what to do. I feel helpless.

"I think she might suspect that the bonus is in jeopardy because I've hinted to her about it. One time in a group meeting, I brought up the topic of bonuses and told a story about how when I worked for another company, many people were upset when they found out that if they didn't hit their target, there really was no bonus. I don't think she got the hint. This is such a hard topic. I dislike disappointing anyone.

"When I think about what I want for myself as an outcome of having direct conversations, I want her to hit the metrics, be successful, and continue to grow as a member of the team.

"What do I want for myself after having this conversation? I want my business to thrive, and I want my employees to be successful."

SELF-COACHING

The NCD Process is not about using communication to get others to behave differently. Rather, practicing the NCD Process increases your self-awareness of thoughts and feelings.

That informs how you react and respond. By increasing knowledge about yourself, you can be in control of how you show up rather than letting your emotions manage you.

There's a tendency, when preparing for a tough conversation, to skip over the process of questioning every thought and feeling you are having. We tend to bring all those thoughts and feelings into the conversation. To be able to self-manage, you must use a self-coaching process to explore the stories your brain generates to protect your self-concept, ego, and feelings so you can leave them aside.

A drive to change the other person can make us forget that we only have the power to change ourselves. It is the other person's journey to determine how they want to respond. Through this self-coaching process, we extend empathy to ourselves.

YOUR TURN: STAGE 1 – WRITE YOUR STORY

Now it is your turn to apply what you have learned to a conversation you know you must have but are avoiding.

On a separate piece of paper, write by hand every detail and thought you have about the conversation you know you need to have. Try to stay within stream-of-consciousness writing rather than crafting a story. Don't censor yourself. Your brain may want to edit out important details, especially those that make you uncomfortable. To get the most out of this process, you need to be comfortable with being uncomfortable and write down every single thought and feeling.

STAGE 2

SIFTING FOR FACTS

OFTEN, we put off having hard conversations for so long, that by the time we take the initiative to talk, the story in our mind has swelled with a mixture of emotion, projections, fears, and blame.

Stage 2 of the NCD Process is the "fact sifter" phase and it's intentionally designed to help you coach yourself through your story. You will start uncovering and understanding the thoughts and fears that make you a hesitant communicator.

When we are ruminating about having a tough conversation, our brain is working overtime creating stories and what-if scenarios. Our brain will interpret those stories as evidence that we are at risk.

In Stage 2, we are not only preparing for this conversation but are also building self-awareness and emotional intelligence. You'll be self-coaching as you sift out everything that is not a fact. By identifying everything that is not a fact, you're learning more about your thinking errors and how they interfere with your communication.

QUESTIONS WE'RE ANSWERING IN STAGE 2

- What emotions or emotional energy are present for you?
- What are your *shoulds*?

- What are your unspoken expectations?
- What assumptions are you making?
- What projections or fears do you recognize in yourself?
- What elements are not a fact?
- What's left?

IDENTIFYING MENTAL HABITS YOU RELY ON

Cognitive shortcuts, heuristics, and biases are the mental habits our brain relies on to process situations and make the easiest and fastest decisions possible. We use these mental habits to problem-solve multiple times per day. Most people are unaware that they're doing so.

Often, they are appropriate and helpful. For example, if I'm working on a deadline and need to get materials printed quickly, I will go to the print shop I've used before. I know them and the quality of their work. They know me and my expectations.

At times, relying on these shortcuts means we're bypassing critical thinking when we need it. Critical thinking may generate a better solution or reveal a long-standing belief that no longer serves us. Shortcuts can mask when we've mistakenly accepted some information as fact. This systematic error in thinking is referred to as a cognitive bias.

Stage 2 is the process of slowing down and looking at your story critically and with curiosity. With practice, you'll increase your awareness of when you are using a mental shortcut. It will help you determine if you're mistakenly relying on a cognitive bias.

Factors that can contribute to our cognitive biases:

- Our emotions
- Limits on our mind's ability to process information

- Social and work pressures

Common Cognitive Biases:

- Assuming others around us share our opinions or beliefs
- Favoring information that confirms our opinions or beliefs
- A tendency to rely too heavily on the first piece of information we learn
- Having our memory about an event or person influenced by what we hear from others
- Estimating that the outcome of a decision will be the same as the last time we used that decision

IDENTIFYING ASSUMPTIONS

Looking critically at your thoughts, can you identify any assumptions you are making? Assumptions that have not been verified or clarified are not facts. When assumptions are left unexamined, it is easy to believe they are facts. It's common to believe that the assumptions we hold are held by the other person as well.

Ask yourself: What are my assumptions in my story? Have these assumptions been clarified, verified, or intentionally shared with that other person?

IDENTIFYING EMOTIONS AND EMOTIONAL HOTSPOTS

Spot the emotions in your story by looking for words that describe how you feel, such as angry, sad, frustrated, anxious, and annoyed.

When we tell ourselves stories about how current events may impact our future, it's called *future tripping*. These stories cause anxiety and activate emotional hotspots, even when we have no evidence that the stories will actually come to pass.

When we are already feeling anxious and we engage in future tripping, our brain sends a signal that we are at risk or need to protect ourselves. This, in turn, drives the fight or flight response and causes us to react in a protective way rather than respond in an intentional way.

IDENTIFYING "SHOULDS"

Look for phrases such as "I should," "They should," or "If it were me I would." Other phrases which indicate that we have a belief about what others should do are "Everyone knows that," or "Anybody would."

It's more important to recognize when you're using cognitive shortcuts than to identify exactly what type of shortcut it is. Identifying them will help you recognize where thinking errors show up in your story. This is how to break the patterns which prevent you from having clean and clear dialogues.

IDENTIFYING FEARS

There is an adage that says, "If you spot it, you've got it." This means that when someone else's behavior really gets under your skin, there's a good chance it reflects something within us with which we are uncomfortable.

Similarly, our expectation of how someone will respond reflects how we would respond if the shoe were on the other foot.

I have learned, from coaching hundreds of people through the NCD Process, that it's rare for the other party in the conversation to have the intensity of emotion that we imagine they will have. Allowing ourselves to be open to whatever their response is will help us have an easeful and fact-based conversation. By putting grace in the space, we can manage our emotional hotspots rather than allowing them to drive us.

IDENTIFYING SHRINKING BEHAVIORS

Shrinking behavior is when we try to withhold or restrict our truth from being said. Shrinking behaviors may range from verbal game-playing to avoiding someone entirely. These behaviors are often unconscious choices that may seem familiar in hindsight.

The most common forms of shrinking are masking, avoiding, and withdrawing.

Masking is when we understate or selectively show our truth. Examples of masking are the use of sarcasm, sugar-coating our truth so it lands softer, hinting, or telling a story instead of the truth.

When we are **avoiding**, we steer clear of a sensitive or uncomfortable topic by talking all around it or diverting the conversation away from what we really feel or need to say.

Withdrawing looks like shutting down the conversation, going silent, or leaving the physical area. It might look loud, like hanging up on someone or storming out of a room. But it can also be subtler, like abruptly changing the topic or moving on to the next agenda item in the middle of a discussion.

AVOIDING THE TRAP OF FUTURE TRIPPING

Future tripping is one of the biggest causes of wasted time, unnecessary drama, and chaos.

Our mind is drawn to engage in future tripping because it feels as if we are actually solving problems and being productive. When we allow our minds to go down this road, we are not focusing on facts that are true now. Instead, we are guessing and making assumptions about what might happen in the future and accepting that as truth. This can lead to creating workarounds or solutions for situations that may not actually occur.

Can you relate to future tripping? We all do it. But left unchecked, it can prevent us from initiating productive conversations we need to have.

Practicing self-awareness is the key to stopping future tripping. Simply pause, take a breath, and be grounded in the facts of what is true right now.

IDENTIFYING UNSPOKEN EXPECTATIONS

Unspoken expectations are another component of our unexamined stories. When we try to hold others accountable to unspoken expectations, it is a setup for confusion, anger, and resentment.

Sometimes, to uncover unspoken expectations, we must reflect a little deeper than on just what we've written. We unconsciously believe everyone should already know our expectations because they often are reflected in the rules, values, or boundaries that we have for ourselves.

Keep an eye out for any expectations that you write down in your story and have not specifically expressed to others or received an agreement on.

IDENTIFYING EXPANDING BEHAVIORS

Expanding behavior is an attempt to convince, control, compel, or force the conversation in the direction we want. Most often these are unconscious or automatic reactions.

The most common forms of expanding behaviors are controlling, coercing, attacking, and labeling.

Controlling manifests as being threatening, demanding, or by gaslighting. **Coercing** manifests as forcing our views on others, interrupting, overstating facts, changing subjects, or dominating the conversation. **Attacking** can manifest in language that is belittling, shaming, or humiliating.

Labeling is often happening inside our minds. For example, we may call another person an idiot or difficult. Labeling also manifests in prejudice. We may think or say phrases like, "All of you people . . .," which groups people under a stereotype or shared description.

Someone exhibiting these behaviors in a dialogue may not appear as vulnerable. But remember that these behaviors are often a sign that an emotional hotspot has become activated.

The only person you can manage is *you* and you can do so by:

- Taking a deep breath
- Grounding your feet on the floor
- Listening for the beat of your own heart
- Sorting out what is fact from what is story

When self-coaching yourself through this process, try to think of the last time you noticed these kinds of behaviors. Were you feeling vulnerable? Were you feeling a need to protect your sense of self, your values, your job security, or how people perceived you?

If you're coaching someone else through this process and you witness behaviors that indicate emotion, simply affirm and ask a curious question such as, "I can see something is happening for you right now. Can you say more about that? Can you tell me more about what's going on?"

IMPORTANT: If someone is suffering any type of harm (physical, emotional, legal, fiscal, etc.), then the situation should be referred to a qualified outside resource such as Human Resources, the police, the legal department, etc.

COMMON THINKING ERRORS

Anchoring Bias: The tendency to rely heavily on the initial information you learned when making decisions or deciding on strategy and to ignore or disregard any factors learned later. It's a good idea to revisit whether the original information, and your interpretation of it, are still true, relevant, and primary. Be willing to change your mind when presented with new evidence.

Escalation of Commitment: A logical fallacy bias where we justify decisions based on the perceived "cost" of time and energy already spent on a person or project, regardless of any new evidence that further investment is imprudent.

Availability Heuristic: The tendency to overestimate the likelihood of events. Can be influenced by how unusual or emotionally charged recent memories may be.

Familiarity Principle: The tendency to prefer what is familiar over what may be new or different. This may be especially relied on when we're feeling rushed, pressured, or vulnerable and can show up as a "should" statement.

Confirmation Bias: The tendency to search for, interpret, focus on, and remember information in a way that confirms one's expectations.

HOW STAGE 2 CAN GO AWRY

In Stage 2, it is important that you trust the process. Your brain will be doing its best work to keep your ego intact and protect you. It is incredibly easy to convince yourself that your emotions, assumptions, fears, and unspoken expectations are valid and necessary.

Your brain may nag you to move on or skip over this stage. Open to the process. Don't judge yourself as good or bad with thoughts like, "I should know better," or "This is embarrassing."

Stage 2 is where you're doing the work of transformation, but it can be uncomfortable. The way out of discomfort is to go through it. You will be glad you did.

LET'S PRACTICE STAGE 2 – AVERY'S STORY

Reread Avery's story. Cross out everything in her story that you believe is not a solid fact. When you finish, you should be left with only the facts. Where do you notice Avery's emotions show up?

Let's highlight the emotions and emotional energy that Avery is projecting onto the conversation she wants to have:

- I'm **afraid** we are going to have a bad quarter if she doesn't hit this goal.
- I'm **really angry** that she isn't holding herself accountable when I know she can do better.
- When I do, I'm **afraid** that she will be so disappointed that she will quit.
- I **fear** she will be resentful and that will cause further headaches.
- **What if** I'm not even cut out to be running this company? I'm so **humiliated** just thinking about that!
- I **feel** helpless.

Where in Avery's story do you see evidence of her cognitive shortcuts? Put a line through all the places where you see cognitive shortcuts being deployed.

Here are a few examples:

- Avery selected a motivational tool that she had successfully used before to motivate this staff person. This is an example of relying on what is familiar instead of doing some additional exploration to try new tools or strategies.

- Avery assumed that she knew how the staff person felt or what they believed about the bonus. Remember, you can only see the world through your own lens. This means that often when we are fearful of people's reactions, we are projecting how we'd react or what we'd feel onto them. Acknowledging our own beliefs, reactions, and feelings allows us to go into the conversation open to any outcome.

As Avery explored her assumption more deeply, she began to wonder if the conversation she needed to have was about getting the bonus or about not meeting the metric. Going through all the questions in Stage 2 helps to get clearer on what the actual conversation is about.

Avery's statement, "I've already invested so much time developing her," shows that Avery believes she must stick with a decision based on time invested, despite new evidence that the decision may no longer be in her best interest.

When Avery realizes that she was considering promoting someone who was already not achieving critical performance metrics, she uncovered a potential pattern of avoidance behavior around decision-making for which she may want to be on the lookout.

A cognitive shortcut shows up in Avery's story as the belief that because a past employee became angry and resentful over not earning a bonus, this employee will do the same. This cognitive shortcut is contributing to Avery's hesitancy to have the tough conversation. Avery has no way of knowing what the staff person is thinking about the bonus.

Another cognitive shortcut shows up when Avery states, "In some ways, she reminds me of me at her age. I really don't want to start over with someone I don't know."

Avery's emotions are very present in her story. She reveals that she feels humiliated when she wonders what others think about her perceived inability to hold this staff person accountable.

This may well be a topic she would want to bring to a coaching session to help her process the emotion and increase her confidence as a manager. But it is not relevant to this conversation with her staff person.

When Avery can cross out the non-facts and irrelevant emotions, she can show up in the conversation with less shame or fear.

In Avery's story, future tripping shows up quite a bit. Avery put a line through each statement that she believed was unproductive future tripping. Here's one example:

> "I'm concerned that if she isn't held accountable, others will wonder why they should work hard to hit their metrics when I can't hold anyone accountable anyway. I will end up with a big problem on my hands if everyone starts slacking and no one is achieving their goals. I could end up losing the whole business. Then what? The idea of that possibility stresses me out so much."

Avery reveals several unspoken expectations in her written story:

- She sees the person as a candidate for a leadership role but hasn't discussed that with the staff person.

- She assumes that the staff person can do better and is simply not holding herself accountable.

- She makes assumptions about what others are thinking or will think.

- She has already formed an expectation about how the staff person will respond and what they will do when she has the conversation.

By identifying assumptions or unspoken expectations, you can see where curiosity and clarifying questions might reveal information that shifts the nature of the conversation. You may even learn that you do not need to have the conversation.

For example, Avery could ask some open-ended, curious questions about what might be blocking the staff person from hitting the benchmarks. Instead, she assumes that she already knows. Her assumptions may have her finding additional ways to provide support or training for her employee. If she asks about the staff person's goals for additional leadership responsibilities, she will find out how the staff person actually feels about a leadership path and, in turn, the benchmarks Avery had set for the staff person.

YOUR TURN: **STAGE 2 – SIFTING YOUR STORY**

Read through your story looking for anything and everything that is not a fact. Circle, cross out, or highlight anything that is an assumption, projection, emotion, or fear. Try to look at your story from an outsider's perspective. Are there unspoken expectations in your story? What remains will be the facts.

Now, look at what remains in your story once you eliminate everything that is not a fact.

- What do you notice?

- What is surprising?

- Do you recognize any pattern or trend in your own thinking or behavior when it comes to conflict with others?

- How did it feel to write out the story in an honest and emotion-filled way?

- How did it feel to intentionally eliminate or cross out your fears, assumptions, and emotions?

STAGE 3

SHAPING THE DIALOGUE

WE BEGIN THIS STAGE by rewriting the scenario using only the facts we uncovered in Stage 2. This is where the conversation begins to turn around and take a new shape.

STAGE 3 IS WHERE THE DEEPER WORK OF NCD OCCURS

You Practice:

- Recognizing your thinking errors and patterns of behavior
- Challenging your beliefs
- Being curious and getting to the facts
- Disrupting your body's automatic reaction to stress

The more often you disrupt your automatic reactions, the more likely you are to change the habits and neural pathways that have been created in your brain over time. You begin to choose how to respond, rather than allowing emotions to manage you.

The power of the NCD Process lies in your willingness and courage to do self-coaching and look deeper into yourself, your thought patterns, and your thinking errors.

HOW STAGE 3 CAN GO AWRY

After Stage 2, we *want* to believe that what remains are the facts. When our ego is threatened, we may have thoughts like, "I feel like I already looked at all the facts. I'm going to bypass Stage 3." **Don't skip Stage 3.**

We're digging deeper to reveal thought patterns, even when it's uncomfortable. It may feel redundant to Stage 2, but trust me, *it is not*. This is the stage where many people are finally able to see deeply held thinking errors and flawed facts. It's typically in Stage 3 that one or two facts are revealed to be irrelevant to the situation or aren't really facts at all.

If you skip over Stage 3, you risk engaging in a conversation that isn't your conversation to have or creating more drama and unhealthy conflict.

When you compare these facts to Avery's original story, you'll see how much less complex and convoluted the information is. Now, we're going to kick the tires on the facts and make sure that every fact is 100% true and relevant.

DIGGING DEEP INTO THE FACTS

Sometimes, in Stage 3, people realize that what they were planning to discuss isn't the *actual* problem. They may also realize that the conversation doesn't need to happen at all.

The Stage 3 questions will uncover any information that has sneakily turned into "facts" in your mind.

While looking at each fact from Stage 2, ask yourself the following questions. If the answer is "No," discard that fact, perhaps by drawing a line through it. If the answer is "Yes," keep that fact, perhaps by circling it.

- Do you know this fact to be true?
- Is this fact absolutely 100% true?

- Is this fact actually your responsibility?
- Is this fact truly relevant to this particular situation?

If you answer "No" to *any of the above questions*, that fact may be flawed.

IDENTIFYING FLAWED FACTS

Sometimes our thinking errors mislead us from knowing what the conversation is really about. In NCD we call this starting with a flawed fact. Frequently, it's not until you've worked through both Stage 2 and Stage 3 that this flaw becomes apparent.

Here's an example from my client, Peter. He had multiple peers come to him with the same complaint about the same manager's poor communication style. Because Peter had known the manager the longest of all the staff, he felt a responsibility to talk to this manager, even though they were not in the same department.

He used the NCD Process to help him prepare for this difficult conversation. He worked through Stage 2 and in Stage 3 finally asked himself, "Is the fact that I have to have the conversation with the manager absolutely 100% true?"

He realized that his story was a perfect example of acting on a flawed fact. It was not his responsibility to talk to the manager. At most, Peter needed to encourage his peers to have a direct, clean and clear conversation with the manager about their concerns.

You might have seen Peter's flawed fact right off the bat. Unfortunately, it's harder to spot our own flawed facts. Sometimes the best course of action is to tell your story to someone else and ask them, "What am I missing here?"

IDENTIFYING AND SETTING BOUNDARIES

You may have heard the saying, "Exceptions to the rule become the rule." When I'm working with people who feel like others are walking all over them, I talk about boundaries and how to uphold them. Every time we set a boundary and then take a step back when someone crosses it, we have created a new boundary.

The first step is to be clear with ourselves about why the boundary is important and worth upholding. Intentional boundaries require attention and tending. But in doing so, we are better able to be healthy, safe, and satisfied.

It is okay to intentionally change or release the boundary. But when boundaries are unintentionally changed, there is room for confusion which leads to conflict and resentment.

Boundaries require us to be emotionally clean and clear in our communication. Many unhealthy conflicts occur not because people don't respect boundaries but because the person setting the boundary did not communicate clearly.

When we are preparing to engage in an emotionally challenging dialogue, we must be clear about our line in the sand. We can't communicate boundaries in a clean and clear way if we don't even know what our boundaries truly are. What is your boundary? Where are you open to negotiating the boundary, and where are you not?

The NCD Process intentionally creates pathways for connection with others. However, some relationships can be quite toxic. Letting those relationships go completely is often the healthiest and most productive way to proceed.

If someone in your life is causing you trauma, physically or emotionally, please seek help from a therapist or counselor to set clear boundaries in ways that protect you.

RELEVANCY AND RESPONSIBILITY CHECK

If you answered "Yes" to all of the fact-checking questions, then ask yourself:

- Does the other person have the ability and resources to change?
- Are the remaining facts relevant? Meaning, do they apply to the other person or the situation?

If you determine that *yes*, the other person can do something with the facts and, *yes*, the facts are relevant, then the final questions are:

- Does this need to be addressed by me? If not me, who?
- Does this need to be addressed by me right now? If not now, when?

DO YOU REALLY NEED TO HAVE A CONVERSATION?

These final questions are not an opportunity to avoid the conversation. Rather, they are designed to help you explore the appropriate timing for the conversation. In some cases, you may discover that this is not a conversation you need to have.

For example: when the person doesn't have the physical ability to make the changes you need, or you're inadvertently taking ownership of a situation that is someone else's responsibility.

If these questions reveal that this is a conversation that you need to have, you are ready to move to Stage 4. If these questions reveal that it is not a conversation you need to have, consider if there is a different action that is appropriate for you to take. There may be a different person you need to speak with, or perhaps there is no further action necessary.

LET'S PRACTICE STAGE 3 – AVERY'S STORY

Here are the facts Avery was left with after completing Stage 2.

- The staff person isn't meeting a key metric.
- Meeting the metric is required to earn a bonus.
- Money is motivating to everyone.
- Whether or not Avery meets the metric is critical for the company to meet their goals
- If the staff person isn't held accountable, others will lose confidence in me as a manager.
- I want to retain the staff person.
- I want the staff person to develop into a leader.

Of Avery's remaining facts, five are 100% true and relevant. The two outliers are, "Money is motivating to everyone," and "If the staff person isn't held accountable, others will lose confidence in me as a manager."

We can't know that those statements are true for everyone without asking them, so we must discard them for this conversation.

Here is what Avery's fact-based story looks like after Stage 3:

> "I have a staff person who isn't meeting a key metric that is critical for the company to meet our goals. As a result, she will not receive her bonus. This is a staff person who I would like to see develop into a leader within the company. However, to do so, she must be able to meet this metric on a consistent basis."

When you compare this fact-based story to what was written in Stage 1, you can see how Avery got clean and clear by working the NCD Process. The Stage 3 version is not only easier to deliver, but it is easier for the staff person to understand, absorb, and respond to.

YOUR TURN: STAGE 3 — SHAPING YOUR STORY

Read through your facts and ask yourself these Stage 3 Questions:

- Are you compelled to have a conversation that isn't even your conversation to have?
- Are you putting time and energy into matters that really aren't yours to resolve?
- In what ways are you trying to do someone else's emotional work for them?
- Do you see patterns in your thinking and behavior? What thinking errors might be bringing this compulsion forward?
- What boundaries might you set for yourself or for others? Are you clearly communicating boundaries?
- Would it be beneficial to be curious, share your thought processes, or convey unspoken expectations?

In addition to exploring these questions, you might explore these topics with a coach. The role of a coach is to help you uncover thinking errors and thought patterns that can hold you back or cause unnecessary hurdles in achieving what you desire for yourself.

STAGE 4

SHARING WHAT YOU'VE PREPARED

THERE ARE THREE PRIMARY THINGS involved in preparing for the dialogue:

1. Listing the facts

2. Identifying your anchor points

3. Being responsible for the energy you bring to the conversation

On a clean sheet of paper, make a list of the facts from Stage 3 so that you can refer to them during the conversation.

HOW STAGE 4 CAN GO AWRY

After you've completed Stages 1, 2, and 3, you may believe, "I've got this. I'm ready to go." But when you sit down to have the conversation, your brain can go blank. The other person's energy, be it defensive or resistant, can take you off course quickly.

Our brains love a plan! Working through Stage 4 is creating a plan that you can execute during the conversation. This relieves stress, worry, and last-minute panic.

Many people complain that they don't want to feel stiff or rehearsed. Stick with Stage 4 and do all the preparation so you (and your brain) will feel confident, relaxed, and prepared. This will help the other person relax their own energy and be more open to listening.

IDENTIFY YOUR ANCHOR POINTS

Your anchor points are your original intentions. You will circle back to these intentions if the conversation goes off the rails, becomes emotional, or loses focus.

To discover your anchor points, go back to your original story and ask yourself:

- What is it that you want for yourself as a result of having this conversation? Write that down in a simple phrase or sentence.

- What is it that you want for the other person as a result of having this conversation? Write down a phrase or statement that articulates this.

- Now identify why having this conversation is in the best interest of the greater good. This can be tricky to pinpoint, but ask yourself, "What will be better served or improved for everyone if I proceed with this conversation." Write this down in a sentence or phrase.

Formulating and rehearsing the anchor points will help you rely on them with ease whenever the conversation drifts off in a direction that is not productive or relevant. Gently reminding yourself and the other person of these anchor points at key times in the conversation can help keep things on track and focused.

LET'S PRACTICE STAGE 4 – AVERY'S STORY

Avery's anchor points were:

- I want my staff person to be successful in her position.
- I want her to grow into a leadership role.
- I want my company to thrive and prosper.

When Avery is in the conversation with the staff person, if she begins to get derailed by the staff person's reaction, she can bring the conversation back into focus by pausing and restating the anchor points.

It might sound like this:

> **Staff Person:** "What do you mean I'm not getting my bonus? Do you know how hard I work? You are unfair. No one else around here works as hard as I do. Is Ron getting his bonus?"
>
> **Avery:** "This conversation is about how I want you to be successful and to grow into a leadership position. Your role is important to the success of the company. And hitting this metric is an essential part of your work."

DIALOGUE CHECKLIST

The more prepared you are, the more confident and calm your energy will be. Being prepared means being clear on the facts, releasing any stories or emotions, putting grace in the space, and being familiar with your anchor points.

Follow this checklist to be fully prepared for your conversation:

1. Before the conversation begins, take a few minutes to balance yourself, be aware of what's happening inside

you, and calm your energy by breathing deeply. Listen for the beat of your heart and imagine it expanding. Picture your heart waves creating a calm and peaceful connection to the other person.

2. Remind yourself of your anchor points which are the outcomes you desire for yourself, the other person, and the greater good.

3. Review the facts so that you can speak your truth, clearly and authentically, without emotional baggage.

4. Here are a few tips to remember:

   - Silence is okay. Pause and put grace in the space for both you and the other person.

   - Choose to be fascinated and curious if you start feeling defensive or angry.

   - Don't get hooked on trying to be right. You and the other person both see things from your own perspective.

   - Pay attention to the energy you bring to the conversation. Breathe and bring yourself back to center if you feel an emotional hotspot becoming activated.

5. Refer to the NCD Principles to remember what steps to take:

   - Be Aware of the Energy You Bring to the Room
   - The Only Person I Can Manage Is Myself
   - Grace is in the Space
   - That's Fascinating
   - Curiosity is the Pathway to Empathy

- You Can Only See the World Through Your Own Lens
- Trust is Built One Conversation at a Time and One Experience at a Time
- At the End of the Day, Everyone Just Wants to Be Seen and Heard

Congratulations! You're now ready to engage in a challenging dialogue.

A FEW THINGS TO LOOK OUT FOR

No matter how well you prepare for a challenging dialogue, if the other person has not also practiced the NCD Process, you may be dealing with someone who is not aware of their own energy. There are some steps that you can take to prevent the reactions of others from knocking you off track.

Crying

People cry for all kinds of reasons. Crying is a very natural release for our physical body. However, we often take the crying we witness in someone else to mean something about us by labeling it.

If someone begins to cry during your conversation, be sure you have some tissues within their reach if they need one. Don't become focused on stopping the crying. It is not about you. Truthfully, you don't even really know what it is about.

If you switch gears to focus on the crying, trying to stop it, or to appease the person, you are shifting away from the facts of what you wanted to discuss.

Of course, you may want to give someone who is sobbing or distraught a few minutes to collect themself. You may even want to employ a coaching prompt such as, "Tell me what you are thinking right now," or "Can you tell me what is happening for you right now?"

Listen to the answer without trying to fix it. Remember, in NCD we start with the belief that people are capable, whole, and able to manage their own emotions. That belief, in and of itself, is empowering.

Blaming

It is not uncommon for someone who is experiencing an emotional hotspot to come back at you listing all the things you've done that they don't like or that have upset them.

When this happens, breathe. Don't allow yourself to go into an emotional hotspot and react. Instead, mindfully respond with an acknowledgment such as, "I hear you have concerns. However, this conversation is about . . . (refer to your anchor points)."

If they continue trying to take the focus away from the topic with blaming reactions, simply repeat the anchor points. I recommend only using this strategy of repeating the anchor points three times in one conversation.

"I hear these are concerns for you. Today we are discussing how the focus of our lives has changed and how we can still maintain our relationship, but in different ways than what we've done in the past."

If you've tried three times to bring them back to the conversation and they are still having a hard time engaging, they may be someone who does better stepping away, reflecting, and returning to this conversation later.

"I think it would be a good idea if we both took some time to reflect and think about this. Let's get together on Friday to discuss it. I'm eager to hear your thoughts and ideas for moving forward because I value our relationship."

Silence

Don't let silence stress you out. Not everyone processes information in the same way or at the same speed. You've been planning for this conversation and the other person is just finding out about it.

Practice getting comfortable sitting in silence. In the facilitation and coaching world, we call this wait time. It allows the other person to acclimate to the setting, get present in the conversation, and collect their thoughts.

In the beginning, the silence may feel like it is quite long. You might be tempted to fill it by repeating what you said, elaborating, giving examples, or asking questions. All that does is distract the other person from the internal work they are doing to get themselves caught up and present.

If it does begin to feel like they've checked out, or are stuck, you can gently use some of the inquiries from the next section.

Feeling Stuck

If you get stuck in the middle of a tough conversation and aren't sure what to do next, breathe, ground your feet on the floor, open your heart, and become curious. Ask an open-ended and simple question. Here are a few of my favorites:

- Can you say more about that?
- Can you help me understand how you came to that decision?
- What would feel helpful to you right now?
- What do you think might happen if you do nothing about this?

When someone answers a question with "I don't know," my favorite follow-up question is, "Can you say more about what it is you don't know?"

Remember, ask the question in as few words as possible and with no agenda and then pause. Breathe. Sit in the discomfort of wait time and silence. Don't reiterate, rephrase, or provide examples. Just lay down a simple, open-ended question, and let it sit between you.

Not every conversation is going to go well or come to the resolution you are hoping for in the time frame that you desire. However, by following the process, preparing yourself, and being aware of where things can go wrong, you will be able to leave the conversation feeling confident and at peace with how you showed up and what behaviors you modeled for others.

PART V

SEEING THE
NCD PROCESS
APPLIED

LORINDA'S STORY

In these chapters, I'm sharing some real-life examples of how NCD has been applied in a variety of situations. I'm always interested to see how each circumstance is unique yet brings up emotions that are familiar. Do you see yourself in any of these stories?

WANTING TO CHANGE SOMEONE'S BEHAVIOR

LORINDA CAME TO TALK TO ME about a problem she was having with her boss. Every time she provided input that was not aligned with her boss or disagreed with him in a meeting, he would get red in the face, start to yell, slam his laptop shut, and storm out of the room.

She wondered what she could do differently to change his reaction. After all, the meetings were about problem-solving and new solutions, so challenging the old way of doing things was an inherent part of the work.

I asked her what she most wanted to say to him. She wanted to tell him how unproductive, unprofessional, and disrespectful his behavior was. As she spoke, she became red-faced, agitated, and tears began to form. Her voice got louder, and she referred to him with labels such as idiot and childish.

By retelling the story, she experienced the activation of an emotional hotspot. This was demonstrated by the physical symptoms that I could see. I asked her what she was feeling in her body right then and if it felt familiar. She indicated that her feelings and physical symptoms did feel familiar. This is how she recognized that when she felt vulnerable or emotionally unsafe, she exhibited expanding behaviors.

I gently asked open-ended questions to help her sort out the facts from assumptions, fears, projections, and emotions. There were a few times when her body language conveyed what I interpreted as frustration and anger.

I asked, "What thoughts are you having right now?"

"I'm really frustrated. I'm regretting talking about this. I want to get up and leave right now," Lorinda said.

At this moment, it was essential that I put grace in the space while taking a deep breath and exhaling, bringing my own energy back to center.

What do you notice about Lorinda's emotional energy? Do you see any similarities between what she states as her desire to get up and leave our session and her boss's behavior of storming out when he feels questioned or challenged?

We all have shrinking and expanding tendencies that are based on our core emotional hotspots.

When I inquired about the desire to get up and leave, I asked if this feeling was something she'd experienced before. She indicated that, yes, she had experienced this in the past.

Often behavioral tendencies that *others* exhibit which leave us feeling the most powerless, upset, or frustrated are ones that activate a similar emotional hotspot within *us*. This mirroring can cause a deep level of discomfort resulting in a desire to act.

Our work together focused on Lorinda's understanding that the only person she can manage is herself. Her boss was going to behave in whatever way he behaved. A conversation with him may or may not change his behavior or increase his awareness of how he is impacting Lorinda. That's okay because the goal is for Lorinda to be able to manage herself in the way that she wants.

Given that truth, my question for Lorinda was, "What do you want to say to your boss?"

She identified three or four key facts about his observable behavior and how it impacted her ability to be productive and for the team to hit their goals. As she prepared her dialogue, she let go of any attachment that what she said would "change" her boss. That is his work. She instead focused on speaking her own truth with empathy and compassion and a focus on the good of the whole.

A few days later, Lorinda let me know that she had the conversation with her boss. She was able to ground herself and proceed with empathy and openness. She stated her facts:

"When you storm out of a meeting, it essentially ends the meeting, and it is hard to regain focus. Forward progress becomes more difficult because, at least for me, it is an uncomfortable situation with lingering impact. I'd like to ask what is happening for you when you do that?"

Lorinda began the conversation with her boss with a statement of fact followed by curiosity. This allowed him to be able to verbalize some of the fears that he was experiencing. Lorinda was able to feel empathy toward him where she previously felt anger and frustration.

I'd like to tell you that everyone was healed and the relationship between them moved forward in a very healthy and positive way. But that's not what happened. What did happen was that Lorinda let go of the attachment to wanting him to be different. She stopped talking about his behavior as if it were personal and about her. She looked at his behavior more objectively. Eventually, Lorinda chose to move on to another position where she did not have to endure her boss's behavior.

The practice of getting clean and clear around your own communication reveals where your own core emotional hotspots are causing you to shrink or expand in response to someone else's hotspots. When this happens, we may feel a drive to change the other person, forgetting that we only have the power to change ourselves. It is the other person's work and the other person's journey to determine how they want to show up.

This is what was happening for Lorinda. She had been so focused on getting her boss to see and acknowledge how wrong his behavior was that she forgot that the only person she can manage is herself. When she regained that perspective through the NCD coaching work, she was able to say what she wanted to say in a clean, clear, and fact-based way, and then make choices for herself.

TONY'S STORY

FEELING PRESSURE FROM MANY DIRECTIONS

TONY IS THE PRINCIPAL of a public school in New England. He traveled to California to learn about the NCD Process and to find out if it would be applicable to improving communication in educational settings.

After he attended his first workshop, Tony contacted me to let me know that he was using NCD daily in his interactions with teachers, other school leaders, and parents. He had received feedback that his ability to manage difficult conversations had greatly improved.

About two years later, COVID-19 hit. Tensions were high. Parents were frustrated and fearful. Teachers were concerned for their own safety as well as uncertain about what remote teaching would look like. And children were having a difficult time processing it all.

The pressures on educators, families, and children were extreme. Every day was a series of challenging, emotional conversations for school leaders.

Tony and I were in touch a great deal. He let me know that he was leaning heavily on the NCD Process to help him have productive, clear, and empathetic conversations, especially when he was feeling stressed, and the other party was feeling vulnerable and defensive.

The need for NCD didn't end when schools reopened, and children and teachers were back in the classroom. Mask mandates, social distancing, and the requirement that children who displayed any symptoms consistent with COVID-19 be sent home meant that Tony's days continued to be filled with hard conversations with overwhelmed teachers and parents. In his words:

"I continued to rely on the NCD Process so that I could have clear, fact-based conversations. I focused on managing my emotional energy even while I knew that I could not control other people's reactions or emotions. NCD kept me grounded, and I know it benefited those around me."

Not every challenging dialogue that you need to have will involve a pandemic or vaccine debate. Sometimes it will be as simple as communicating that you won't be at a family function or as complex as giving feedback to an underperforming employee.

NCD is not for every conversation. We all have hundreds of conversations per day that aren't emotionally challenging. NCD is for the conversations you know you must have or want to have but you resist because you fear what the reaction might be.

(RAYMOND'S STORY)

BUILDING TRUST

RAYMOND WAS A PLUMBER who had a contract for a very large home construction project. Between the time he gave his proposal and the start of the job, the COVID-19 pandemic started. Prices for materials skyrocketed as they became harder to obtain. The homeowner had also added some features and upgrades that weren't included in Raymond's original pricing.

Raymond assumed that, of course, the homeowner would understand that all of these factors would increase project costs. But when he finally discussed the costs, the homeowner got upset. He felt blindsided and sought out second opinions on the cost of the job. His trust in Raymond was negatively impacted.

Raymond conveyed that he thought they had developed a solid working relationship, almost a friendship. He was not only offended by the reaction of the homeowner but was also unsure if he even wanted to continue the job. He asked me, "How can I avoid this happening again?"

When I asked if he felt that he had done his best to communicate in a fact-based way and that the client had heard him, Raymond thought for a moment and answered "Yes, I do."

This coaching was taking place within a workshop. I could see by the look on the other participants' faces that no one was buying that Raymond believed his own words. At that moment, however, I validated him by saying, "I believe you."

This was a pivotal moment in our communication because Raymond was feeling very vulnerable. It was clear he had decided (consciously or not) to approach the pricing discussion with his client in a casual and offhand way. But in his mind, he had been direct and clear about pricing.

When someone is feeling vulnerable or at risk like Raymond was during our work together, they are likely to believe exactly what they are telling you, no matter how illogical or untrue it may seem to you. This is because their amygdala is telling them to protect themselves.

I wanted to engage in a productive, emotionally clean and clear conversation with Raymond because he had asked for my help in sorting this out. However, it was going to be difficult to move forward with him if I challenged his belief that he had communicated in the best possible way.

So, instead, I told Raymond, "I believe you" to convey that I believed his belief. He then gave an audible sigh of relief. I could see his facial features relax, and he began to offer alternatives to how he might have approached the situation.

"I guess, maybe, I could have set up a formal meeting specifically to talk about pricing and how costs were being impacted both by the pandemic and by upgrades," he said. "I just didn't want to upset him."

Circumstances were now quite different than before the pandemic. Raymond acknowledged that as he took on larger, luxury home jobs, perhaps he needed to have a more formal approach with clients around pricing than he had in the past.

When we debriefed as a group, the other participants identified the moment when I told Raymond that I believed him as the doorway to when he went from being angry at the client to looking at himself.

Believing someone else's perspective is a way of honoring their truth in that moment. By remembering that at the end of the day everyone just wants to be seen and heard, I was able to provide a safe space for Raymond. In turn, he was able to unblock the thinking errors he used to protect himself but were ultimately getting in his way.

When you feel vulnerable or at risk, your amygdala goes into protection mode. You are more likely to become defensive, justify your actions, or place blame on others. When you are in protection mode, you are less open to new perspectives, ideas, and possibilities. When you feel heard or believed, the amygdala can take a break from trying to keep you safe.

Great communicators intentionally validate and acknowledge where people are at with statements like, "I hear you," "I believe you," and "I understand this is your perspective." The reason we hesitate to affirm or validate others is that we have a belief that in doing so, we are giving up or surrendering our own truth. This is not the case.

By rethinking how we communicate, we work toward a place where I can accept your truth as being valid in this moment, let you know that I do, and still also hold my own truth without having to try to convince or manipulate you to see the world as I do.

Although this shift in perspective may seem simple, it takes a great deal of practice to truly question what your mind is insisting will keep you safe. The fact is, holding on out of fear of releasing old beliefs doesn't protect you at all.

Living life with curiosity and openness to different perspectives creates more connection with others. Being connected through healthy, honest, and empathy-filled relationships means we are far more protected.

For three years, I had the privilege of working for a Native American organization helping to codify curriculum, develop a leadership team, and work with tribes and bands across North America to implement programs. One day an Elder said to me, "Beth, if you want to win a tug of war, let go of the rope."

It sounded so simplistic then, but I've carried this with me as a reminder since. Whenever I find myself defending a belief so tightly that I am engaging in conflict over it, I remember these words, "Let go of the rope." When I let go of the rope, it doesn't mean that I win by having victory over another. I win because now I'm open to new opportunities, learning, and innovations in a way that wasn't possible when being a winner or loser was the only outcome.

When working with Raymond, I simply let go of the rope. What the observers felt was that release of tension. Raymond was then able to step into creating new possibilities for himself, his work, and his communication with clients.

SHASTA'S STORY

STRENGTHENING CONNECTION

So many people who originally learn the NCD Process for application in their work tell me wonderful stories about the positive impact the tools have on their relationships with the children in their lives. Shasta's story touched my heart.

"I went for a hike with my 11-year-old son recently," she said. "As we were walking, instead of just talking back and forth, I used the curious questions I learned in the training to engage with him. We had a great conversation, and I learned so much about him and his thoughts. They were some of the best hours of my life!"

As adults, we spend too much time telling children what they should think, feel, and believe. We do this because we want them to learn from our experiences and avoid discomforts, disappointments, and heartaches like the ones we've felt. The result is that children grow up thinking that most adults don't hear them or understand them.

The next time you are in the company of a child, pause from being the expert and simply listen. Instead of responding with statements, respond with curiosity:

"Oh, say more about that."

"That's so interesting. Why did you choose that?"

"How did you feel when that happened?"

"What do you think you might do next?"

You might just experience the best two hours of your life and learn a bit along the way.

BETH'S STORY

A MERCURIAL MANAGER

When I began teaching NCD I was hired by a Board of Directors to work with the Executive Director of their agency. She was considered very successful. She had a long history of keeping the budget in the black, managing expenses, and running very successful, high-profile events. However, the board was fielding multiple complaints from her staff and some of their consumers regarding her emotional outbursts and behaviors that could be categorized as bullying.

When I was present in their office, I noticed that staff often asked their co-workers about the weather. The frequency was odd, and the answers didn't always align with what I saw happening outside the window. Some of the things I heard:

Question: "Hey, does anyone know what the forecast is for this afternoon?"

Answer: "I feel like it could be stormy."

Question: "What's the weather look like?"

Answer: "Nice and sunny today."

To help me better understand the culture I did a series of confidential interviews with staff. One of the staff members revealed that the Director's moods were so unpredictable that the staff had developed a system to check in with each other on her mood. They asked each other what the weather forecast was. Sunny meant it was a good day to approach her with a question or new idea. Stormy meant try to stay out of her way because she was not in a good mood.

The team was expending a lot of effort to navigate the emotional energy of their leader, and that level of navigation is necessary all too often in workplaces and in families.

I worked with the leader and team to incorporate NCD into their culture. Soon, positive communication and healthy conflict became more prevalent, and the "weather reports" stopped being necessary.

PART VI

SUSTAINING YOUR PRACTICE

THE NCD MANTRAS

PRINCIPLES TO GUIDE YOU

Rachel took one of the first NCD workshops I ever led back in 2009. She's moved jobs since then, but we've stayed connected. She continues to tell everyone about NCD and how much it has benefited her professionally and personally.

We were talking via Zoom one day when she showed me a poster she had made for her office wall. On the poster were the NCD Mantras. "I keep these right in front of me because if I start to get pulled into drama, those mantras remind me to use the tools of NCD," she said.

The mantras are the principles of NCD.

Throughout this book, I've been using the mantras as guideposts for the NCD Process. Each mantra is a simple saying that acts as a reminder to let the NCD Process guide you.

The more you practice the mantras, the more they will be integrated into how you show up as a communicator who listens, is empathetic, and holds space for others to be fully seen and heard.

I even find myself using mantras to stop my brain from spinning stories. When I catch myself playing a scenario over and over, or feel emotions start to bubble up, I can tell myself, "That's Fascinating", and that's enough to break the cycle.

The mantras are:

- Be Aware of the Energy You Bring to the Room
- The Only Person I Can Manage is Myself
- Grace is in the Space
- That's Fascinating
- Curiosity is the Pathway to Empathy
- You Can Only See the World Through Your Own Lens
- Trust Is Built One Conversation at a Time and One Experience at a Time
- At the End of the Day, Everyone Just Wants to Be Seen and Heard

SURPRISE DIALOGUES

A DIFFERENT CONVERSATION

WE'VE SPENT OUR TIME in this book discussing planned dialogues. A *surprise dialogue* is any kind of conversation or interaction where you are totally caught off guard and feel the symptoms of emotional hotspots. Surprise dialogues are as likely to happen in a meeting as they are in the grocery store or at a family dinner.

The first step is to put grace in the space. This is the best way to clear out the emotional hotspot so you can think clearly and plan a response. Step two is to focus on the facts rather than a story.

Responding, instead of reacting, to a surprise dialogue takes practice and self-awareness. As you become skillful with the NCD Process, you will find these interactions easier to manage.

RESOURCES

SUPPORTING YOUR PRACTICE

I've created some materials to help you get started and keep building your NCD practice. You'll find these on my website at **NCDsolution.com/ttcafiles**.

- The NCD Process Worksheets are the complete self-coaching framework for working through your tough conversation. Please download and use these worksheets the first few times you prepare a conversation. Eventually, you will find yourself using the questions automatically without needing the worksheets because you have internalized the process.

- When you feel an emotional hotspot being activated and you want to return to center, try listening to the Heart Expansion visualization. You can download the recording to your own device. Once you listen to this brief visualization a few times, you will be able to follow the steps and guide yourself to a place of balance and centering anytime and anywhere without the recording.

- Print the poster of the NCD Mantras. Many people keep a copy of them in their office, workspace, or in their home to serve as a reminder of the key concepts and principles of NCD.

IN CLOSING

WHERE WE GO FROM HERE

THE NCD PROCESS is a self-awareness practice. Once you are familiar with NCD, you won't be able to ignore it. You will see applications for the NCD Process everywhere you look.

While you can share your observations with others, they too will need to go through the experience of learning the NCD process to experience the benefits.

Hundreds of people who've been trained in the NCD Process have contacted me with stories of how the conversation they were dreading went far better than expected. They are grateful for the tools of the NCD Process.

I hope that you experience the same freedom.

Share this book and the tools widely so that we can live in a world where everyone can navigate challenging dialogues in an emotionally healthy, clean and clear way.

Welcome to the NCD Movement!

ACKNOWLEDGMENTS

SPECIAL THANKS to my life partner, Janet, and my daughters, Lily and Annie. I am grateful for your belief in me and your support.

This book would not have been possible without the help of an amazing group of generous and skillful people who volunteered to read and give honest and clear feedback so this book could be readable, enjoyable, and useful. I'm so grateful to each of you: Amy Burford, Claudia Hall Christian, Karen Crane, Patti Digh, Lisa Faulkingham Hunt, Betsey Nash, Jen Ottinger, Todd Simendinger, and Colleen Watters.

Thanks, also, to Ginger Moran, developmental editor. Ginger's framework, expertise, and coaching made an overwhelming process simpler and much more doable.

Andrea Buchtel has walked with me on the path of bringing this book to life for over five years. From the first day we met, and I gave her an overview of NCD, Andrea was on board to help me bring it into the world in a bigger and more cohesive way. She has done all the heavy lifting that it takes to bring this book to fruition. I am eternally grateful for her skillfulness, commitment, vision, confidence, and intuition. I've relied on each of these throughout this journey.

ABOUT BETH WONSON

BETH WONSON lives in Sacramento, California with her partner, Janet, her horse Bailey, and her dog, Gracie.

Beth is a speaker, leadership coach, and facilitator. She loves sharing the magic of NCD with audiences of all sizes and in all industries. In addition to doing work she loves, Beth enjoys the ocean, the redwoods, creating art, and spending time with family and friends.

You can reach Beth at support@ncdsolution.com.

www.ingramcontent.com/pod-product-compliance
Lightning Source LLC
Chambersburg PA
CBHW050417120526
44590CB00015B/2003